Strategic Learning in the Content Areas

Doris M. Cook
Consultant
Reading Education

Wisconsin Department of Public Instruction
Madison, Wisconsin

This publication is available from:

Publication Sales
Wisconsin Department of Public Instruction
Drawer 179
Milwaukee, WI 53293-0179
(800) 243-8782
www.dpi.state.wi.us/pubsales

Bulletin No. 9310

ISBN 1-57337-015-0

© 1989 Wisconsin Department of Public Instruction
Revised and approved for reprint 1991, 1995, 1997, 1999, 2004

Printed on Recycled Paper

Contents of the Guide

10 Appendixes

In Wisconsin, we make it a priority to help classroom teachers at all levels fulfill their responsibility to teach reading and writing strategies that are essential to learning in content areas. *A Guide to Curriculum Planning in Reading,* and other guides in various disciplines, were developed by Wisconsin educators to provide practical applications of the most recent research in learning. All guides stress the across-the-curriculum importance of reading and writing as learning tools. Wisconsin curriculum guides have been well received by educators and are used throughout the United States and in some countries around the world.

This publication continues to help classroom teachers become knowledgeable and effective in educating students as strategic learners. Designed to augment our curriculum guides in all subject areas, it also can provide support for college- and university-level preservice training and serve as a resource for staff development.

Wisconsin is a recognized national leader in reading education. Our publications continue to disseminate cutting-edge research on reading. Our teachers gain a richer understanding of the reading process and foster development of growing numbers of independent, strategic learners. And, most importantly, our students benefit from effective, research-based instruction.

Elizabeth Burmaster

Elizabeth Burmaster
State Superintendent

Acknowledgments

Strategic Learning in the Content Areas would not have been possible without the efforts of many people. Members of the task force freely gave their time and expertise in drafting the guide. In addition, their employing agencies generously granted them time to work on the publication. The task force members are

Doug Buehl
President-elect
Wisconsin State Reading Association
Reading Consultant
East High School
Madison Metropolitan School District

Leslie McClain-Ruelle
School of Education
University of Wisconsin-Stevens Point

Diane Hein
Reading Consultant
Cherokee Middle School
Madison Metropolitan School District

Richard J. Telfer
College of Education
University of Wisconsin-Whitewater

Nancy Hoth
Certified CRISS Trainer
PreK-8 Reading Coordinator
Kaukauna Area School District

Doug Vance
State Coordinator
International Reading Association
Reading Consultant
La Follette High School
Madison Metropolitan School District

Nancy Kavasch
Curriculum Coordinator
West Bend School District

Rosalind Wold
Reading Consultant
Wisconsin Rural Reading
  Improvement Project
Education Department
Viterbo College
La Crosse

The members of the task force decided at the beginning that they wanted this guide to be state of the art and to reflect the rich understanding of the reading and learning processes that research has provided.

To that end, the task force worked diligently and efficiently to translate this body of knowledge into a practical and workable format for classroom teachers. In the years ahead, they hope to see much of the content reflected in school programs and practices.

In addition to the task force, many other people contributed to the guide. Sincere thanks and appreciation goes to Beau Fly Jones, program director at North Central Regional Eductional Laboratory in Elmhurst, Illinois. She served as the project consultant and provided constant support throughout the development of the guide. Many of her ideas are reflected in the text. The earlier studies she conducted with Friedman, Tinzmann, and Cox; the framework she developed with Palincsar, Ogle, and Carr; and the synthesis and application paper she wrote with Pierce and Hunter were all valuable resources. We are indebted to all these researchers who explored the complex thinking processes that enable all students to become strategic learners.

I also wish to thank the following consultants from the Bureau of Program Development in the Wisconsin Department of Public Instruction who contributed to "The Content Areas" section of this guide: Chet Bradley, Donald Chambers, Kenneth Dowling, David Engleson, Frank Grittner, Michael Hartoonian, Gordon Jensen, Ellen Last, Mel Pontious, and Martin Rayala.

I also appreciate the assistance of the vocational education consultants in the areas of Agriculture Education, Business Education, Family and Consumer Education, and Technology Education. We hope they will find the guide useful in working with their content-area teachers.

Margaret Wilsman, manager of research for Wisconsin Public Radio and Television and codirector of the Wisconsin Rural Reading Improvement Project, was always available for consulting and reviewing drafts. Many of the innovative contributions in this text are being tried or have been initiated in the Rural Reading Improvement Project.

I would also like to thank Media Support Section Chief Greg Doyle; text editors Patricia Braley, Bill Chickering, Elizabeth McBride, and Paul Zelewsky; graphic artist Victoria Rettenmund; and photographer Neldine Nichols for their valuable contributions to this guide. Their patience and assistance are sincerely appreciated.

A special word of thanks also goes to Connie Haas and Patricia Venner for their help in preparing the manuscript. Thanks also to the quick and accurate work done by the Word Processing Center: Danni Jorenby, Bev Kniess, Deb Motiff, and Theresa Post.

Many of the ideas in this guide represent the accumulated knowledge of the teachers in the schools represented by the task force. We look forward to seeing these teachers model the strategies discussed in its contents.

Doris M. Cook
Supervisor, Reading Education

There is growing evidence that reading and writing instruction should continue with increasing sophistication beyond the elementary grades and should be incorporated into every content area. Data from the National Assessment of Educational Progress (NAEP) indicates that 61 percent of our 17-year-olds may have difficulty learning effectively from high school textbooks (Reading Report Card, 1985).

Research in strategic learning indicates that students can learn from textbooks if they are shown how. Further, recent reports from the International Reading Association Secondary suggests that the responsibility for teaching reading and writing strategies essential to understanding and learning the appropriate content belongs with classroom teachers.

The purpose of this publication is to assist teachers at all levels and in the content areas to help students become independent strategic learners.

Users of this guide will need to refer often to *A Guide to Curriculum Planning in Reading,* published by the Wisconsin Department of Public Instruction, which establishes the basis for this document.

Note that both the reading guide and this guide are based on the philosophy that with proper instruction students can understand the reading/learning process and apply this knowledge across the curriculum (see *A Guide to Curriculum Planning in Reading,* Figure 2 and pp. 18-25). Both documents emphasize that learners continuously develop and refine the ability to

- construct meaning from text,
- apply strategies to learn from text,
- develop interests and attitudes that encourage reading for pleasure as well as for the life-long pursuit of learning.

The emphasis given these three goals of instruction will vary according to the stages of developmental growth described in the curriculum guide. Even though all three goals are treated at every developmental stage (see *A Guide to Curriculum Planning in Reading,* pp. 16-20), each stage is characterized by its own particular curricular emphasis, which varies according to the complexity of the texts, the vocabulary, the tasks, and the readiness of the learner.

The ability to activate prior knowledge when acquiring new vocabulary or concepts and the ability to organize information into meaningful frameworks for understanding and remembering are crucial to successful learning. This guide will illustrate some of the demands required of students as they read content materials for specific tasks. Strategies designed to aid learning from content texts are also included.

While many of the strategies presented in the guide are appropriate for all content areas, specific applications will vary among content areas because of the nature of the materials and the tasks. Model lessons are suggested for the specific application of strategies appropriate for certain content areas.

This publication addresses the need for teachers to view reading and writing as important learning processes across the curriculum. It challenges many traditional notions about purposes of content-area instruction. Educators are challenged to view teaching as more complex than simply delivering content. While content is critical, effective instruction should enable all students to become successful, independent learners. To accomplish this, all teachers are encouraged to address two goals: the learning of content and the development of independent learners.

This guide is intended to be the basis for a staff development program. An effective staff development program can help school districts achieve a successful content-area reading program that develops independent learners. Teachers at all levels and all disciplines will find many useful techniques. Reading specialists can use the contents as the foundation to organize a series of effective inservice sessions and as they collaborate with classroom teachers, to model new instructional techniques. Principals and superintendents will find the guide helpful as they work with reading specialists to develop systematic, long-term staff development programs that support and encourage teachers to experiment with new instructional approaches. University and college instructors can use it in courses designed to meet the new certification standards.

By using this information along with *A Guide to Curriculum Planning in Reading*, content-area teachers can be the catalyst for change in their schools. They can promote the process that will help all students become strategic learners.

Reading Redefined: Implications for Content-Area Learning

1

The concept of reading as an interactive process, with readers bringing meaning to the page as much as getting meaning from the page, is now accepted in the world of practice as well as research.
—NAEP (1988)

Introduction

The current research on reading and cognitive learning has helped us acquire a much richer understanding of the reading process. The definitions of reading in *A Guide to Curriculum Planning in Reading* (Wisconsin Department of Public Instruction, 1986) and in *Becoming a Nation of Readers* (1986) describe reading as a constructive and strategic process. The Wisconsin Model for Reading Comprehension (*A Guide to Curriculum Planning in Reading*, p. 10) depicts reading as an interactive process in which factors related to the *reader*, the *text*, and *context* influence comprehension. The key to this new definition is that the reader constructs a meaning rather than merely reproducing a meaning from what is seen on the page. The four conditions that determine what meaning a reader will construct from a text are as follows:

- what the *reader* brings to the reading situation,
- the characteristics of the *text*,
- the learning *context* that defines the task and purpose of the reader as well as the setting, and
- the *strategies* applied by the reader to obtain meaning.

Readers are guided by their purpose and the background knowledge and experience they bring to the reading task. These factors, plus the nature of text, influence the strategies the reader needs to employ. Comprehension is determined by the learner's effectiveness in using the strategies to construct meaning. The Wisconsin Model will be applied throughout this book as the guide for planning and implementing content-area reading instruction for developing strategic learners.

Reader/Learner

To construct meaning, the reader interacts with the text and bridges the gap between the known and the new knowledge. Prior knowledge is the key for new learning both from text and verbal messages as new information is linked with prior knowledge.

Central to this publication is the analogy of a strategic reader as a strategic learner. The DPI's *A Guide to Curriculum Planning in Reading* defines a strategic reader as one who is in charge of his or her reading, analyzes the reading task and reading material, makes an appropriate plan for achieving the purpose, and then monitors his or her understanding while reading.

Strategic learners are in charge of their reading and learning. They are concerned with constructing meaning as they draw upon a variety of strategies. Recent research defines the strategic learner as highly en-

Figure 1 ■

Wisconsin Model for Reading Comprehension

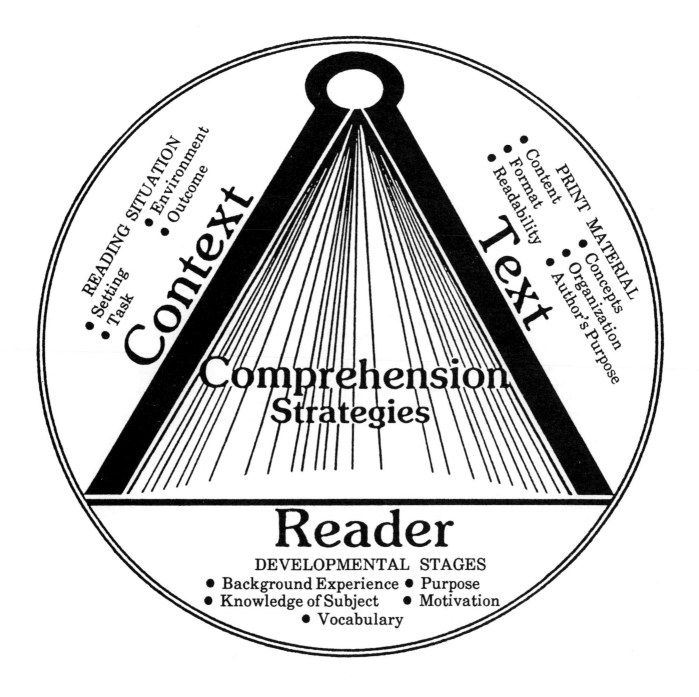

gaged in thinking processes oriented toward four purposes: to construct meaning, to understand, to solve problems, and to become independent learners. The essence of learning is linking new information to prior knowledge. It is relatively new in educational theory to conceptualize learning as thinking, that is, as using prior knowledge and specific strategies to understand the ideas in a text (Jones, Palincsar, Ogle, and Carr, p. 5). Chapter 3 describes the content-area learner as an active strategic learner who uses prior knowledge to learn new information.

Text

Another integral component of the Wisconsin Model is text. Text characteristics play a significant role in learning. Students who understand text structure have increased comprehension and better recall of information. Text characteristics include vocabulary, density of information, conceptual level, organizational patterns, and graphic representation. Texts clearly organized and well-written are called considerate text, while poorly written texts are referred to as inconsiderate.

Although text comprehension is strongly influenced by the reader's background knowledge and experience, texts have a structure separate from the reader's cognitive structure. Therefore, it is especially important that students are taught to recognize and use text structure for organizing their learning. Chapter 4 demonstrates a variety of frames and graphic representations that teachers and students can use to identify the author's underlying organizational structure. Model lessons using these frames for specific content areas are presented in Chapter 8.

While most content-area instruction is based on the use of a single textbook, teachers are increasingly using supplementary materials, such as trade books, periodicals, reprints, and literature. We strongly encourage this wide use of reading material.

Context

Context, another component of the Wisconsin Model for Reading Comprehension, is critically important for helping students become strategic learners. Context includes environment, setting, task, and outcome. Each of these areas affects the strategies the learner draws upon. Environment refers to the classroom atmosphere, which is a combination of peer attitudes, teacher's expectations, and the home environment. Setting refers to the physical place and conditions under which the instruction and learning take place.

The question often arises as to where and when content-area reading instruction should occur. *Becoming a Nation of Readers* specifically suggests "that the most logical place for instruction in most reading and thinking strategies is in the content areas." The strategies presented in this guide are most useful when the student grapples with important content. We consider the content-area classroom as the ideal context for instruction in content reading and have written this guide especially for content-area teachers.

Context also includes the task and the outcome, which together determine the purpose for reading. The teacher's expectations for a specific reading assignment determine the way a student approaches a specific task. Does the reading need to be carefully examined for mastery of details or will a general understanding of the major ideas suffice? Will the information be tested or discussed? Will the reading be used to complete a worksheet, answer questions, write an essay, or carry out a lab experiment? Different outcomes require different learning strategies.

Each of these contexts for learning and for developing strategic learners are explained in Chapter 5.

Strategies

Strategies refer to cognitive activities learners can use to bring meaning to a task. There should be a clear relationship between the strategy selected, the task, and the text. The challenge for the learner is to choose the appropriate strategy for the task.

Researchers are continually identifying and validating diverse strategies that encourage independent strategic learning. These strategies are used in the following ways:

- to motivate students and help them focus attention,
- to organize information for understanding and remembering,
- to monitor learning.

This guide refers to teaching and learning strategies. Teaching strategies are techniques teachers model and use to help students become independent, strategic learners. These strategies become learning strategies when students can independently select the appropriate one and use it effectively for accomplishing a task. Strategies need to be taught as means for effective learning, not as ends in themselves.

Since strategies taught outside a specific content area do not transfer, this publication will address the uniqueness of each content area and offer appropriate strategies.

Reading comprehension is not a set of subskills that can be taught in isolation of conceptual objectives; rather, the processes of learning need to be integrated into idea related instruction.

Instruction

If students are to become strategic learners in content areas, they need instruction in what strategies are available, how and when they work, and how to determine if their strategies are helping them learn. Direct instruction and modeling are two effective ways of developing students' ability to know how and when to apply strategies to specific text. These instructional approaches will be addressed later. In addition to direct instruction and modeling of appropriate strategies, students need guidance, support, and coaching throughout the reading process. The teacher's role in helping students learn *how* and *when* to use a strategy is a major concept emphasized throughout this publication.

Chapter 6 suggests a dual role for teachers of content areas. Besides being subject matter specialists, teachers also must model and demonstrate the thinking that goes with effective learning so students can become strategic learners, A model for strategic teaching, offered in the framework in Figure 4, encourages instructional decision making by the teacher throughout all stages of planning and instruction.

Research Evidence and Classroom Implications Pertaining to Strategic Learning

2

The past two decades have seen considerable change in accepted assumptions about reading instruction in American schools. Recommendations for good teaching include moving from an overwhelming emphasis on basal readers and workbooks toward a greater emphasis on comprehension strategies, a wider range of higher-quality reading materials, more independent reading, and more opportunities for combining reading and writing activities.
—NAEP (1988)

Introduction

A considerable body of research supports the process shown in the Wisconsin Model for Reading Comprehension. This chapter presents the research evidence and identifies implications from that research. The evidence and implications are organized around the features of the Wisconsin Model: the learner, the text, and the context. The final section in this chapter focuses on staff development. Specific strategies mentioned here (such as PReP and DRTA) are explained in detail in Chapter 9.

Table 1 ■

Research and Implications Pertaining to the Learner

Statement: Students get more out of reading when their background knowledge is activated or when the teacher elicits, builds, and focuses appropriate background knowledge.	
Research Evidence	**Classroom Implications**
In general, the more students know about a topic, the better students comprehend and learn from text on the topic. In fact, background knowledge is the strongest predictor of student ability to make inferences about text (Adams and Bruce, 1982; Rumelhart, 1980; Stevens, 1980).	Assess students' background knowledge about the topic to be studied through activities such as brainstorming and discussion activities such as LINK (List, Inquire, Note, Know). ● Activate students' background knowledge through activities such as KWL Plus (Know, Want to Know, Learned) and PReP (Pre Reading Plan). ● Build background knowledge through direct instruction, demonstrations, audiovisual presentations, field experiences, hands-on activities, discussions, and conceptual mapping. ● Guide students in predicting what they will read about through questions, Anticipation Guides, and DRTA (Directed Reading Thinking Activity).
Students benefit from prior knowledge about the form and organization of the content (Armbruster and Anderson, 1984; Bartlett, 1978).	Preteach the patterns or frames of organization for the expository texts being used. ● Help students analyze the organization of passages in the text. ● Teach narrative structures and story grammars for narrative texts.
Since vocabulary knowledge and performance on measures of reading comprehension are highly correlated, vocabulary instruction that focuses on relating new words to known concepts appears to have the best effect on the acquisition of word meaning and improvement of comprehension (Beck, Perfetti, and McKeown, 1982; Johnson, Toms-Bronowski, and Pittelman, 1981; Schacter, 1978).	Select and preteach important vocabulary and relate concepts to the students' background knowledge through Vocabulary Overview Guides and the Frayer Model.

Research and Implications Pertaining to the Learner

Statement: Students get more out of reading when their background knowledge is activated or when the teacher elicits, builds, and focuses appropriate background knowledge.	
Research Evidence	**Classroom Implications**
Student misconceptions about subject matter may inhibit learning and may result in "true" explanations falling on deaf ears (Schoenfeld, 1985; Anderson and Smith, 1984).	Anticipate students' misconceptions about the topic and preteach appropriate concepts.

Statement: Successful learners use their knowledge of text features and appropriate strategies to monitor their own progress.	
Research Evidence	**Classroom Implications**
Successful learners are aware of task demands, text features, and appropriate strategies (Brown, Campione, and Day, 1981; Flavell, 1978).	Teach effective strategies to help students become aware of text features and task demands. ● Model effective strategies through read alouds and teacher-led discussions. ● Encourage students to discuss their use of strategies in learning.
Successful learners monitor their own comprehension and adjust their learning strategies accordingly (Paris, Lipson, and Wixson, 1983; Brown and Palincsar, 1982).	Teach students to monitor their comprehension and ask, "How am I doing?" ● Encourage students to stop when comprehension breaks down and to adjust their strategies.
Successful learners generate relationships among parts of texts and between text and their prior knowledge (Wittrock, 1983; Linden and Wittrock, 1981).	Lead students to generate relationships among ideas through modeling, semantic mapping, graphic organizers, questioning, and teacher-led discussions.
Successful learners are effective problem solvers (Carpenter, 1985; Schoenfeld, 1985).	Teach problem-solving strategies with an emphasis on formulating questions as well as finding solutions. ● Provide learners with a wide variety of problem-solving situations including real-world problems.

Table 1 (continued) ■

Research and Implications Pertaining to the Learner

Statement: Students who are actively involved in their learning are more effective than students who play a more passive role.	
Research Evidence	**Classroom Implications**
Students who generate questions, make summaries, and help determine the direction of the lesson are more effective learners than students who do not (Cohen, 1983; Brown, Campione, and Day, 1981; Kintch and Van Dijk, 1978; Andre and Anderson, 1978-79; Frase and Schwartz, 1975).	Use teaching techniques that maximize student involvement and improve student ability to listen, question, and discuss in large and small groups—techniques such as the Reciprocal Teaching or Re Quest strategies .
Students who write about what they are reading comprehend and remember more than students who merely read (Myers, 1984; Moffett and Wagner, 1983).	Provide time for students to write as they read. ● Expect students to summarize what they have read. ● Teach students how to take notes and have them do so in a variety of class situations.

Statement: There is a positive correlation between learning, self-concept, and positive attitudes.	
Research Evidence	**Classroom Implications**
Teachers who value reading and learning tend to produce positive attitudes and high achievement in their students (Edeburn and Landry, 1976).	Model a love of learning and reading while teaching. ● Read aloud. ● Share personal interest in new knowledge and learning.
Students with high levels of reading achievement tend to have high self-concepts, and vice versa (Quandt and Selznick, 1984).	Teach strategies for learning that build student confidence and achievement as independent learners.
Success tends to enhance student self-concept (Johnston and Winograd, 1985; Quandt and Selznick, 1984).	Build positive student attitudes and self-concepts through careful material selection and techniques that foster student interaction and student success.

Statement: Successful learners use effective memory strategies.	
Research Evidence	**Classroom Implications**
Memory is related to background; those who know more are able to remember more (Pauk, 1984; Bradsford et al., 1980).	Activate and build appropriate background knowledge.

Research and Implications Pertaining to the Learner

Statement: Successful learners use effective memory strategies.	
Research Evidence	**Classroom Implications**
Short-term memory is limited in capacity (Peterson and Peterson, 1959; Miller, 1956).	Review main concepts frequently and use techniques that build student understanding of relationships between ideas and concepts. ● Provide graphic representations of main concepts to be learned.
Most of what is learned is quickly forgotten if it is not acted upon (Loftus, 1980; Doctorow, Wittrock, and Marks, 1978; Craik and Lockhart, 1972; Bower, 1970).	Teach students specific techniques for remembering concepts effectively, including notetaking, guided reading/lecture procedures, notecards, imagery, meaningful organization, and association. Teach students to construct graphic representations for thinking and remembering.

Table 2 ■

Research and Implications Pertaining to the Text

Statement: Students have difficulty learning from content-area materials because of the nature and structure of these materials.	
Research Evidence	**Classroom Implications**
Because content-area materials are predominantly expository, students who have learned to read using primarily narrative material are exposed to new and unfamiliar patterns of organization (Bereiter and Scaramalia, 1982; Meyer, 1979; Marshall and Glock 1978-79; Bartlett, 1978).	Teach students how to read a variety of expository text materials.
Expository text structure differs from subject area to subject area and there are different patterns of organization within a text (Jones, Palincsar, Ogle, and Carr, 1987; Meyer, 1985; Frederiksen, 1975).	Model effective strategies for reading expository text that students can apply in content-area learning, such as Graphic Outlining. Teach students how to identify and use text patterns or frames as aids to comprehension.
Statement: Reading difficulty is affected by a number of features within the text.	
Research Evidence	**Classroom Implications**
Reading difficulty is affected by the amount of prior knowledge the author assumes the reader possesses (Rumelhart, 1980; Spiro, 1980; Anderson, 1977).	Select texts that match as much as possible students' background knowledge and reading ability.
Reading difficulty is affected by the amount of new content presented in the text (Nagy, Herman, and Anderson, 1985).	Adjust instruction to accommodate the concept load of the text.
Reading difficulty is affected by the degree to which the text can bridge the gap between the content knowledge possessed by the reader and the content and structure of the text (Herman et al., 1985).	Use learning strategies that help students bridge the gap between reader and text.
Reading difficulty is affected by the degree to which the text explicitly represents the structure of the content being presented (Armbruster and Anderson, 1984).	Teach students to recognize different text structures.
Reading difficulty is affected by inconsiderate text, which is obscure, incoherent, unstructured, and poorly organized (Anderson, Armbruster, and Kantor, 1980).	Teach students strategies for dealing with poorly written text. ● Model and teach comprehension monitoring strategies. ● Teach students to reread, look ahead, and what to do when comprehension fails.

Table 3

Research and Implications Pertaining to the Context

Statement: Prereading instruction leads to improved comprehension, recall, and motivation.	
Research Evidence	**Classroom Implications**
Setting a purpose for reading aids comprehension (Kintch and van Dijk, 1978).	Help students to set their own purposes for reading. ● Use Re Quest, KWL Plus, and brainstorming as important prereading strategies.
The perspective taken by the reader determines what is identified as important and what is remembered (Anderson and Pichert, 1978; Anderson et al., 1977).	Teach students to take a point of view as they read. Use strategies such as Reading from Different Perspectives.
Prereading questions aid comprehension when seeking specific information (Goetz et al., 1983; Fass and Schumacker, 1981).	Provide students with questions and encourage self-questioning. Provide adequate guidance so students turn headings into questions and use preview or summary questions as prereading.

Statement: The opportunity for students to interact with other students leads to increased achievement and motivation.	
Research Evidence	**Classroom Implications**
Cooperative learning strategies have led to increased achievement as well as to improved interpersonal relationships (Dansereau, 1987; Palincsar and Brown, 1985; Slavin, 1980, 1982).	Teach students to work cooperatively in large and small groups.
Students tutoring other students can lead to improved achievement for both the student and tutor (Cohen, Kulik, and Kulik, 1982).	Balance teacher-led discussions with classroom activities that foster positive student interactions. ● Encourage study groups, paired learning, and peer tutoring.
Teacher-led discussions are often question-answer sessions and are not interactive (Durkin, 1978-79).	Model and implement strategies that foster cooperative learning in groups.

Table 3 (continued) ■

Research and Implications Pertaining to the Context

Statement: Questioning affects comprehension.	
Research Evidence	**Classroom Implications**
Students learn more effectively when they generate their own questions (Andre and Anderson, 1978-1979).	Use Reciprocal Teaching, Re Quest, DRTA, and other teaching strategies to teach students how to generate their own questions as they read.
Students who are exposed to higher-order questions understand more than students who are exposed only to lower-order questions (Wixson, 1983; Redfield and Rousseau, 1981; Anderson and Biddle, 1975).	Ask more high-order questions as part of discussions, class activities, study guides, and tests.
Teachers tend to ask questions that require only literal recall of information and ask those questions in a rapid-fire fashion, as many as 150 questions per hour (Gall et al., 1975).	Allow more time for students to respond to questions.
Students tend to give more thoughtful, reflective responses to questions when teachers allow more time for responses and encourage follow-up (Tobin, 1987; Fagan, Hassler, and Szabo, 1981; Rowe, 1978).	Ask students to elaborate and define answers.
Students learn more effectively when they ask questions about the text organization.	Teach students to ask questions about text structure before they read and as they read.

Table 4

Research and Implications Pertaining to Staff Development

Statement: A systematic, long-term program of staff development is needed if significant improvement in teacher behaviors is to take place.

Research Evidence	Classroom Implications
Staff development is a central part of the total effort of a content-reading program (McClain-Ruelle, 1988; Vacca, 1986).	Include continuing staff development as part of the content-reading program.
Teachers are not the only personnel who can benefit (Vacca, 1986).	Involve administrators and other support personnel in reading staff development.
Four components of training that "virtually guarantee the successful implementation of almost any approach include theory, demonstration by others, practice and feedback, and coaching" (Joyce and Showers, 1980, 1982).	Plan staff development training to include the following components: • theory, • demonstration, • practice and feedback, and • coaching.
Coaching is the key to the effective transfer of training from workshop to the classroom (Sparks, 1986; Showers, 1984).	Provide opportunities for teachers to work with mentors (other teachers and support personnel) to facilitate transfer to the classroom.
With coaching, most teachers will begin to use newly acquired skills in classrooms (Showers, 1984).	Encourage continued application and evaluation of newly acquired skills.

The Strategic Reader/Learner

3

Prior knowledge can account for more variation in reading performance than either I. Q. or measured reading achievement.
—Johnston and Pearson (1982)

Introduction

Content-area teachers recognize that students come to a subject with a variety of backgrounds, attitudes, and abilities that affect their class performance. One student may talk a good game, another may be highly motivated to go beyond the subject, and a third may sit quietly but perform brilliantly on tests and in writing. Teachers also recognize those among non-achievers who can perform but don't and those who simply cannot handle the material.

The perception of the content-area reader as learner has changed dramatically. This change stems from an increased understanding of the process of comprehension. Until recently teachers believed that if a student could decode the words, the student could comprehend. Therefore, a great deal of emphasis was placed upon reading the words and little emphasis was placed upon comprehension.

Learning occurs when new information is integrated with prior knowledge.

Decoding, however, did not guarantee comprehension. Attention then shifted to an examination of the types of questions asked. Taxonomies were developed for discussing the questioning techniques used in the classroom. However, simply asking questions at a variety of levels did not guarantee comprehension.

In the late 1970s, borrowing upon theory from cognitive psychologists, researchers in learning began to explore the effects of the learner's prior knowledge on comprehension. They determined that prior knowledge plays a major role in comprehension of reading materials. In addition, research into developmental differences in readers has revealed metacognitive differences in reading behaviors (Flavell, 1978). Students who use their metacognitive abilities, that is, monitor how they know and what they know, are better readers than those who read without self-awareness (Brown, 1980; Flavell and Wellman, 1977). Since such monitoring requires a reader to take an active role in the process, reading is seen as an active process. The effective content-area reader is described as an active *strategic* reader. In addition, a *positive* self-concept can have a *positive* effect on a student's reading and learning performance. These evolving views have dramatically changed our understanding of the content-area learner. Furthermore, with careful use of the new research, we can improve poor readers' abilities by helping them become active strategic learners and readers in all content areas.

Prior Knowledge

The more students already know about their subject, the better they perform. Teachers also see that students do better later in the semester as they become adjusted to the style and organization of the textbook as well as the way the teacher presents and tests the material.

Extensive research exploring the benefits of prior knowledge on comprehension has consistently indicated that students who have relevant prior knowledge comprehend material far better than those who do not (Tierney and Cunningham, 1984). This factor plays a greater predictive role than traditional measures when assessing reading comprehension performance. "Prior knowledge can account for more variation in reading performance than either I.Q. or measured reading achievement" (Johnston and Pearson, 1982).

Prior knowledge can be considered in three categories. One is knowledge about the topic. Topic knowledge needs to be relevant and accurate. Both good and poor readers who approach a new topic with misconceptions have an extremely difficult time adjusting their prior knowledge to include the new information (Capper, 1984). Thus, prior to instruction, it is important to determine if the student knows anything about the topic and if the knowledge is appropriate. Once misconceptions are identified, comparisons must be made with the misconception and new information. Finally, it is imperative that misconceptions are corrected.

Prior knowledge is crucial and necessary for new learning.

A second type of prior knowledge, knowledge about text structure and organization, requires students to be familiar with narrative and expository forms of writing. Researchers have noted that middle-grade students' ability in reading declines as predominantly narrative formats shift to textbook or expository formats. When students know text structure, they can read and comprehend material better than when they are faced with new, unfamiliar patterns. In addition, readers who can perceive the organization of the material and who use this organization for structuring learning will read and comprehend material better than those who cannot.

A third type of prior knowledge is word meaning. The vocabulary used in content areas can be general or content-specific. Readers familiar with vocabulary terms used in material comprehend better. Those who possess strategies perceiving word meaning in context are better able to handle unfamiliar material.

The reader's prior knowledge of topic, text structure, and word meaning must be considered before asking students to read or learn about new material. The significant point is that when a reader has the opportunity to activate a knowledge base and build prior knowledge, the reader achieves positive gains in reading comprehension.

Metacognition

Content-area teachers often recognize that students struggle because they do not know how to learn and remember the material, and further, the students are not even aware that they do not know. If only the learning strategies of the best students could be taught to all of the students the job of the content-area teacher would be much easier.

The term *metacognition* refers to an awareness and understanding of one's learning process (Flavell, 1978). The metacognitive process in reading includes self-knowledge, task knowledge, and self-monitoring. Self-knowledge involves recognizing strengths and weaknesses in comprehension. Task knowledge requires matching a comprehension task with an appropriate learning strategy. Successful readers actively monitor their comprehension (Baker and Brown, 1984). Rather than being passive receivers of content, they continuously check to see if they understand, if the new information fits with what they already know, and if they agree with the author's message. These readers actively seek the meaning of the material and its relevance to them.

Since the poor reader focuses on isolated words rather than the meaning of the whole, he or she is not aware that interaction should occur between the text and the reader. On the other hand, the good reader knows to use "fix-up" strategies when something in the reading does not make sense and knows how to make adjustments to correct the problem. The poor reader has no such strategies to draw upon, uses inappropriate strategies, or does not realize the need for strategies. The significant point is that when a reader is trained in self-monitoring skills and fix-up strategies, the reader finds positive gains in independence and reading performance (Baker and Brown, 1984).

> *It is clear that we can train the cognitive skills for comprehending and studying texts even with students who would be regarded as recalcitrant by many teachers.*
> *–Baker, Brown*

Learning Strategies

> *One cause of students' difficulties has been the emphasis on teaching reading as a series of discrete skills isolated from each other and from the process of reading.*
> *–Michigan*

Learning strategies refer to techniques used to enhance understanding and memory of the material being learned and read. Good readers set purposes for their reading. They determine a reason for reading selected materials, while poor readers tend to read without direction, without purpose. Poor readers passively read without considering how to approach the material. Good readers identify strategies that will assist them in remembering the material. These strategies involve active manipulation of the content such as rehearsal, summarization, or questioning. Good readers integrate new information with existing knowledge structures. Poor readers are unaware of successful learning strategies and merely attempt to add the new information to their memory rather than integrate the information into their knowledge structures (Jones, Palincsar, Ogle, and Carr, 1987). The significant point is that when a reader is trained to establish a purpose and actively use a repertoire of learning strategies, the reader finds positive gains in reading performance (Baker and Brown, 1984).

Self-Concept

In general, good readers possess a positive self-concept and a sense of control in regard to their reading performance. Good readers attribute success to their own efforts. Successful readers use self-monitoring, self-instruction, and reanalysis of the task when they encounter failure. Poor readers tend to attribute any success to luck and have little control over their reading performance (Jones, 1987). When poor readers fail, they attribute it to a lack of ability, thus beginning a cycle of learned help-lessness. It is understandable that a passive reader who lacks background knowledge, self-monitoring skills, and appropriate learning strategies would express a lack of control. Teachers may reinforce this feeling by supplying answers and making excuses for the "helpless" reader. The significant point is that a reader's self-concept is amenable to change and providing feedback for those experiencing low self-concepts can assist in bringing about change.

Strategic readers monitor their understanding of text.
–Paris, Brown

New Insights

Understanding the reader as an active, strategic learner has evolved within the last five to ten years. *A Guide to Curriculum Planning in Reading* (1986) presents a definition and explanation of the strategic reader. We are gaining new insights into the processes used by effective readers and are using these insights to help less effective readers. This guide focuses on how the development of readers in areas such as prior knowledge, metacognition, and learning strategies can bring significant gains in reading performance. We now have the knowledge to help our readers become effective, strategic learners in content areas.

Table 5

Metacognitive Behaviors of Good and Poor Readers

Mature/Good Readers	Immature/Poor Readers
Before Reading	
Activate prior knowledge	Start reading without preparation
Understand task and set purpose	Read without knowing why
Choose appropriate strategies	Read without considering how to approach the material
During Reading	
Focus attention	Are easily distracted
Monitor their comprehension by • knowing comprehension is occurring • knowing what is being understood	Do not know they do not understand
Anticipate and predict	Read to get done
Use fix-up strategies when lack of understanding occurs	Do not know what to do when lack of understanding occurs
Use contextual analysis in order to understand new terms	Do not recognize important vocabulary
Use text structure to assist comprehension	Do not see any organization
Organize and integrate new information	Add on, rather than integrate new information
After Reading	
Reflect on what was read	Stop reading and thinking
Summarize major ideas	Feel success is a result of luck
Seek additional information from outside sources	
Feel success is a result of effort	

Learning from Text

4

Subject matter textbooks pose the biggest challenge for young readers being weaned from a diet of stories.
–Becoming a Nation of Readers

Introduction

The word *text* refers to all printed matter used in the classroom, including textbooks and supplementary materials. Of these materials, the textbook is still the major tool for organizing and presenting information in content-area classrooms. More than 90 percent of instruction is based on textbooks.

Many students find it hard to learn from textbooks because they lack adequate background knowledge of the subject or are unaware of text structures. Others have difficulty because they feel the content is uninteresting or irrelevant to their lives. Poorly written or poorly organized textbooks also can cause problems.

In the past, teachers have compared a text's readability score, which usually is based on sentence length and vocabulary level, with what they know about students' reading abilities to determine how difficult a textbook would be for their students to understand. This method, however, is too simplistic.

Reading is more than the literal interpretation of words and sentences. This guide views reading as an interactive process during which readers construct meaning according to their purpose, background knowledge, motivation, and perceived task or outcome. For example, students who have no knowledge of American Indian culture other than what they have learned from television westerns will comprehend a text on American Indians very differently than students of Indian heritage or students who have visited Indian reservations.

Teachers who have spent years learning a subject often cannot understand why students have problems with textbooks. They fail to realize that a book that seems to them to be clear and logical may make little sense to students unfamiliar with the subject.

Text Organization: The Key to Understanding

Every day, as they move from classroom to classroom, students in the upper grades encounter six or more learning environments, each requiring a different set of reading tasks. Yet most students approach every reading assignment in the same way. Teachers can help students cope with the demands of each subject by teaching them how to recognize and use the organizational patterns in textbooks.

Authors choose organizational patterns, called text structures, that will best express their ideas. Knowledge of text structures allows readers to identify the hierarchy of an author's ideas and select the most important points of a passage.

In well-written textbooks these patterns are easily identified. The most common are description, proposition/support, sequence, compare/contrast, problem/solution, and conflict/cooperation. Often a reader can identify a text structure by noting specific signal words. For example, "therefore" and "for this reason" indicate the author is using a problem/solution structure; "similarly" and "on the other hand" signal a compare/contrast structure.

Frames are sets of questions or categories of information implied by a particular text structure. Students can use frames to pull out information essential to understanding the material they are reading. Frames are not in a text but in readers' minds. Graphic representations, such as time-lines and spider maps, help students identify particular frames.

A text may have several different organizational patterns, and good readers apply a different frame to each to understand the information presented. For example, a student would use a cause/effect frame when reading about the effects of drugs, shift to a compare/contrast frame to understand the differences between drugs, and then use a problem/solution frame when engaged in a discussion about solutions to drug abuse problems.

According to Jones, Palincsar, Ogle, and Carr (1987), some frames are generic. For example, the problem/solution frame can be found in many disciplines.

Other frames are specific to a content area. The region frame, for example, is concerned with surface features, weather conditions, landmarks, and products. Skilled readers with some knowledge of geography are aware that these categories of information are likely to be found in geography textbooks. Similarly, a skilled reader would expect to find information about a character's goals and attempts to achieve those goals in a story or documentary.

There are three categories of frames. They consist of those that apply to texts

- containing one major element or idea and supporting information
- describing a sequence
- containing two or more important elements or ideas

The types of organizational frames to be used with texts containing only one major element are description, proposition/support, argumentation for a conclusion, and concept/definition. The organizational frames to be used with texts describing a sequence are sequence and goal/action/outcome. Lastly, the compare/contrast, problem/solution, cause/effect, and interaction organizational frames work well with texts containing two or more important elements or ideas.

When students construct graphic representations of text they read, students better understand which ideas in the text are important, how they relate, and what points are unclear.
—Jones, Pierce, Hunter

Texts Containing Only One Major Element or Idea and Supporting Information

Description. Descriptive frames and categories depend somewhat on the nature of what is being described. For example, description in literature focuses on characters, places, and objects. In such descriptions, readers must identify what is being described and its attributes. In geography, regions are usually described using such categories as land, people, and government. Descriptive texts are sometimes referred to as list or collection structures because the attributes may be described in any order.

Descriptive Graphic Structures

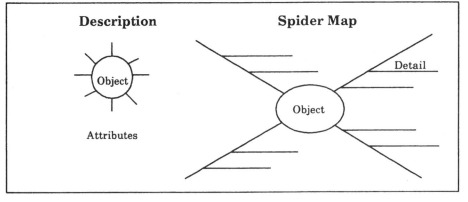

Signal Words

also	further	moreover
and	furthermore	too
besides	in addition	

Frame Questions

What is it?
Where can it be found?
What does it look like?
What are its attributes?

Proposition/Support. Proposition/support is a very common paragraph structure. In its most simple form, it is a statement plus information supporting the statement. Frame categories for a theme paragraph, for example, include the statement of the theme, elaboration and interpretation of the theme, and supporting information, such as examples, quotes, and data. Proposition/support paragraphs often have both major and minor supporting ideas.

This structure is sometimes difficult to identify because it uses few easily recognizable signal words.

Proposition/Support Graphic Structure

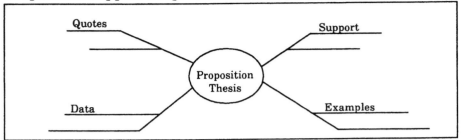

Signal Words

accepting the data	granted that	of course
for example	suggest	indicate
above all	more important	indeed

Frame Questions

What is the proposition/thesis?
How is it supported?

- Examples?
- Quotes?
- Data?

Argumentation for a Conclusion. This frame also provides for varying degrees of complexity. Simple arguments contain only two categories of information: the statement of a conclusion (an opinion or action) and premises (reasons, examples, facts, quotes, etc.) that support the conclusion. More complex argumentation frames also contain complex chains of reasoning and explanations of the reasons. The critical task in comprehending an argument is evaluating the logic linking the premises to the conclusion. This includes questioning the adequacy of the information and the quality of reasoning.

Argumentation Graphic Structure

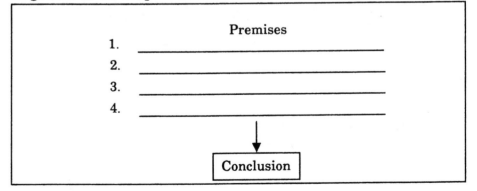

Signal Words

for these reasons	if	then	so that
in conclusion	therefore	hence	

What is the conclusion?
What are the arguments for the conclusion?
What are the premises that support the conclusion?

Concept/Definition. To understand a concept, it is important to know what it is, what category it belongs to, and its critical attributes. Readers also must connect new concepts with what they already know by using examples, analogies, or comparisons.

Concept/Definition Graphic Structures

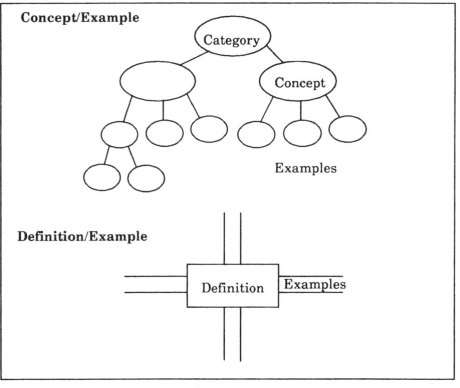

Signal Words

for example	specifically	as	which is
e.g.	for instance	such as	like

Frame Questions

What is the concept?
What category does it belong to?
What are its critical attributes?
How does it work?
What does it do?
What are its functions?
What are examples of it?
What are not examples of it?

Texts Describing a Sequence

Sequence Texts. An important task when reading sequence texts is understanding and predicting the correct sequence of events. Events in sequential structures may be in chronological order or some other logical order. Typical sequential texts are steps in a procedure (e.g., how milk is pasteurized) and stages of development (e.g., the life cycle of primates). Literature and history texts involve flashbacks and forecasts.

To understand sequential texts, readers should identify the object, procedure, or initiating event; describe the stages, steps, or series of events that follow, showing how one leads to another; and describe the final outcome.

Sequential Text Graphic Structures

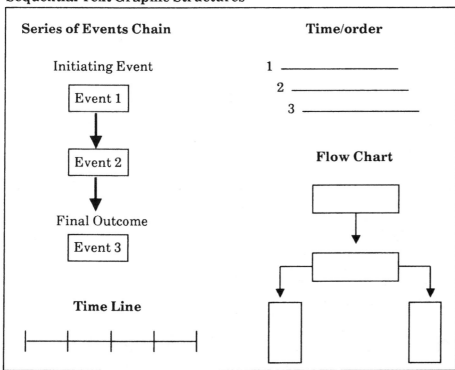

Signal Words

finally	second	then	to begin with
first	next	last	later
afterwards	meanwhile	now	previously
before	subsequently	presently	ultimately

Frame Questions

What is the subject or object?
How did it begin?
What are the steps/stages?
What is the outcome?

Goal/Action/Outcome. Much of human behavior in literature or any narrative is goal-oriented (e.g., winning despite a handicap or surviving under difficult circumstances). A useful way to summarize goal-directed behavior is to identify the goals, actions, and outcomes of the person or group depicted in the text. Clearly, there is a sequential component in goal/action/outcome frames; often, however, the goal is not obvious early in the text.

Goal/Action/Outcome Graphic Structure

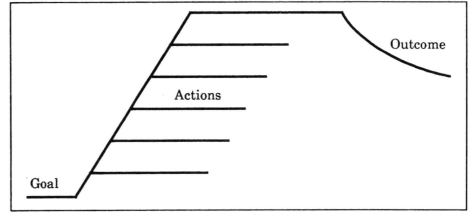

Signal Words

if	although	unless
providing	whenever	

Frame Questions

Who are the characters?
What is their goal?
What are the actions?
What is the outcome?

Texts Containing Two or More Important Elements or Ideas

Compare/Contrast. Compare/contrast structures identify the points that are being compared, the ways in which they are similar, and the ways in which they are different. Sometimes the structures include a summary statement indicating the points compared are more alike than different.

One can organize compare/contrast structures in different ways: one can present the whole set of similarities followed by the whole set of differences; one can make point by point comparisons of the similarities and differences; and one can mix these two patterns.

Compare/Contrast Graphic Structures

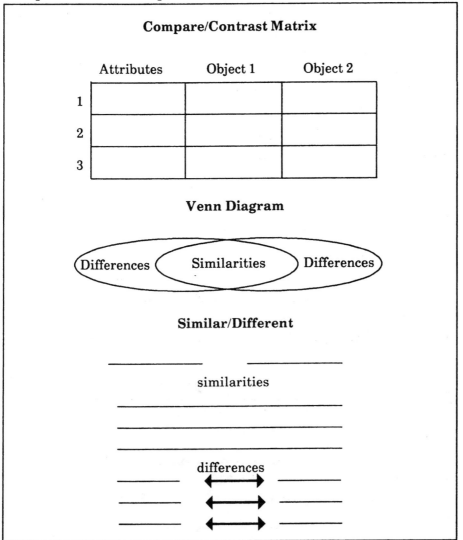

Compare/Contrast Matrix

	Attributes	Object 1	Object 2
1			
2			
3			

Venn Diagram

Differences — Similarities — Differences

Similar/Different

_____   _____

similarities

_____

_____

_____

differences

_____ ⟷ _____

_____ ⟷ _____

_____ ⟷ _____

Signal Words

as well as	at the same time	similarly
equally important	likewise	while
but	on the contrary	still
conversely	on the other hand	though
despite	yet	nevertheless
however	regardless	whereas

Frame Questions

What are the elements?
How are they alike?
How are they different?
What is the conclusion?

Problem/Solution. Most problem-solving frames pertaining to people in fiction and history focus on identifying who had the problem, the general definition of the problem, its causes and effects, actions taken to solve the problem, and the effects of the actions. Such frames also may contain elements of decision making, such as defining available options, resources, and the consequences of acting on each option. Problem/solution frames for literature may focus on how characters look for solutions and why they choose certain solutions. Problem/solution frames also have a sequential component.

Problem/Solution Graphic Structures

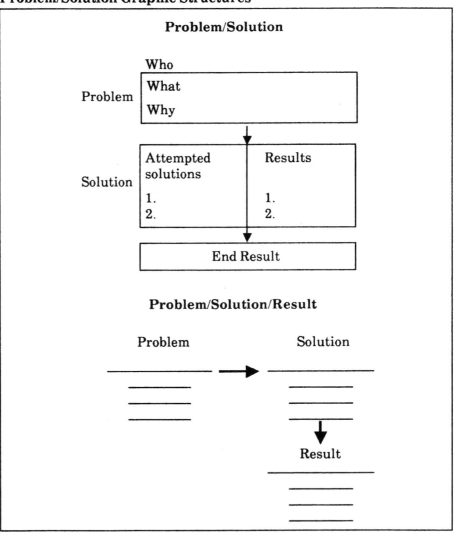

Signal Words

because	although	in spite of
for this reason	even though	either/or
therefore	unless	neither/nor
instead of	instead of	rather than
notwithstanding	otherwise	

Frame Questions

Who has the problem?
What is the problem?
What is causing the problem?
What are the negative effects?
Are there any positive effects?
What actions are taken to solve the problem?
What are the consequences?
What further problems result?

Cause/Effect. These frames involve establishing an effect and its cause or causes. Often they explain how causes are linked to effects. Complex cause/effect frames may involve a sequential chain of causes and/or interaction of various factors as well as multiple effects. These frames are sequential; however, descriptions often begin with effects and then discuss causes.

Cause/Effect Graphic Structures

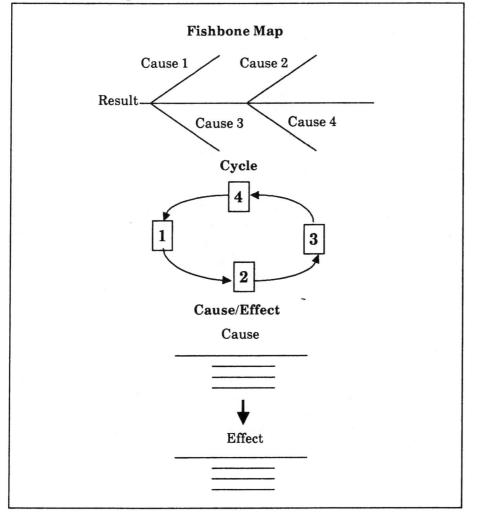

Signal Words

accordingly	since	then	so that
because	so	thus	as a result
consequently	hence	therefore	if . . . then
for this reason	this leads to	nevertheless	

Frame Questions

What is the effect or result?
What are the causes?
What are the factors that cause x?
Which ones are most important?
How do the factors interrelate?

    Interaction (Cooperation and Conflict). Most literature involves the interaction of two or more persons or groups (e.g., the interaction of a child and an animal or a child and his or her parents). Interaction frames contain both sequential and compare/contrast structures.

Interaction Graphic Structure

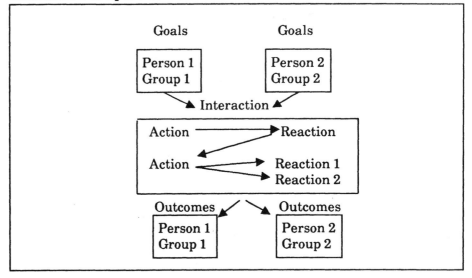

Frame Questions

Who are the persons/groups being depicted?
What are their goals?
What is the nature of their interaction: conflict or cooperation?
How do they act and react?
What is the outcome for each person or group?

Many students have problems learning from text that lacks study aids, is badly written, or is poorly organized. Armbruster and Anderson (1984) call such text *inconsiderate*. Because traditional readability formulas only measure sentence length and vocabulary difficulty, they do not always identify inconsiderate text or indicate why students might have difficulty reading it. Consequently, teachers must examine text carefully for those features that help or hinder students' learning.

Poorly organized text is often hard to follow. It does not clearly state main ideas, contains too much superfluous information, and does not show logical connections. On the other hand, considerate text presents important information in clearly identified organizational patterns.

Teachers often fail to recognize inconsiderate text because they are familiar with its content. They need to keep in mind that their students lack most of the background knowledge needed to understand the vocabulary, concepts, difficult pronoun referents, and allusions.

Students often fail to see causal connections when they are not explicitly stated. When authors omit important signal words, such as "therefore," "most important," "first," "second," and "last," students may have trouble following the organization. Ironically, textbooks that have been "dummied down" to meet readability requirements are actually more difficult for students to read because they leave out these important connectives.

Sentences that rely on complicated syntax, passive voice, or inverted sequence also cause problems. And while sentence length alone does not make text difficult, students do have trouble with text that contains many long, difficult sentences or all short, choppy ones. Vocabulary density also can negatively affect comprehension, especially if new words and concepts are not defined.

Headings and titles should provide students with a clear outline of the material. Pictures and captions should relate to the text. Introductions, purpose statements, and prequestions should help students activate prior knowledge and set a purpose for reading. Postreading activities should encourage students to think about what they have read and help them integrate new information with existing knowledge.

What can be done when teachers find that texts being used are inconsiderate? The obvious solution is to select a new text. Before a textbook is purchased, teachers should evaluate its considerateness and try it out with students. Sample 1, on the following page, provides an assessment checklist for such an evaluation.

However, purchasing new texts is not always possible, and teachers often must help students cope with the inconsiderate texts they are issued. Teachers can teach students effective strategies for learning from poorly organized, poorly written text. Teachers can help students create their own frames for organizing important information. They also can model effective coping strategies by reading aloud and explaining how they are able to learn from inconsiderate text.

Textbook Assessment

Title:_____

Author:_____

Publisher:_____

Copyright:_____

This checklist is designed to help you evaluate the considerateness of the textbook you are using or considering purchasing for your class. A considerate text helps students learn. An inconsiderate text places roadblocks in their path.

As you evaluate the textbook consider students' background knowledge. You may want to ask students to help evaluate the text.

Using the following scale, evaluate how well the text meets the criteria listed.

Inconsiderate				**Considerate**
1	2	3	4	5

Look at the whole book.

_____ Does the overall content of the text reflect what you feel are the important concepts in your course?

_____ Is the content up to date and relevant to your students?

_____ Does the book contain helpful organizational features such as a table of contents, index, glossary, and appendices?

_____ Is the book clearly organized?

Look at each chapter.

_____ Is a helpful introduction provided for each chapter?

_____ Is sufficient background knowledge provided so that students can link new knowledge with information previously learned?

_____ Is there a clearly recognizable organizational pattern for each chapter?

_____ Is the organizational pattern signaled by headings, transition words, bold print, italics or other indicators?

_____ Do the questions and activities draw attention to the organizational pattern of the chapter?

_____ Do the questions encourage thoughtful responses?

_____ Does the text suggest activities for students to practice using new concepts?

_____ Do the pictures, graphic aids, and supplementary information clearly relate to the important concepts of the chapter?

_____ Are there summaries that clarify the organization?

Examine the way the book is written.

_____ Does the textbook use clear, readable language?

_____ Is the level of vocabulary appropriate for the background of your students?

_____ Does the text introduce new vocabulary clearly using direct definitions or examples?

_____ Is the vocabulary density (i.e., percentage of difficult words) appropriate for your students?

_____ Are the assumptions about prior knowledge of the content appropriate for your students?

_____ Does the text clearly explain new concepts using concrete examples that link the concepts to what students already know?

_____ Is the level of sentence complexity appropriate for your students?

_____ Does the text use active verbs and personal pronouns such as "you," "we," and "us" to involve the students in the content?

_____ Does the text clearly link pronouns to referents and place subjects and verbs near the beginning of sentences?

_____ Does the text stick to the topic and avoid irrelevant details?

_____ Does the text relate content to students' lives?

_____ Does the text provide positive models for both sexes and for different ethnic or cultural groups?

Look at the teacher's manual.

_____ Does the teacher's manual provide introductory activities that build on students' background and motivate them to read?

_____ Does the teacher's manual provide guidance in helping students recognize organizational patterns?

_____ Does the teacher's manual provide follow-up activities that help students integrate new knowledge into existing frameworks?

Look at supplementary materials.

_____ Do supplementary materials, such as texts, worksheets, or computer programs, support the concepts presented in the text?

_____ Are supplementary materials motivating and interesting?

Weaknesses

On which items was the book rated lowest?

What are the weaknesses of this text?

What can you do in class to compensate for the weaknesses of this text?

Strengths

On which items was the book rated highest?

What are the strengths of this text?

What can you do in class to take advantage of the strengths of this text?

Irwin, J.W., and C.A. Davis. "Assessing Readability: The Checklist Approach." _Journal of Reading_ 24 (1980), pp. 129-130.

Supplementary Reading Materials

Many textbooks do not encourage higher-level thinking. Instead, they present readers with isolated facts and predigested conclusions. For this reason, many teachers use supplementary materials to present their subject. Audiovisual and computer programs build background knowledge and spark student interest. Custom-designed handouts provide up-to-date information, present diverse viewpoints, and foster interactive learning. And many teachers find that students who read periodicals, literature, or nonfiction trade books related to the field, such as biographies and how-to manuals, are more interested in the subject and understand it more deeply. Table 6 presents a grid of alternative reading materials for different fields of study.

Table 6 ■

Supplementary Reading Materials

Subject Area	Newspapers and Magazines	Research Materials	Symbolic Materials	Problem-Solving Materials	Trade Books	Primary Sources
Social Studies	Current events Controversial issues Feature articles Political news	Encyclopedias Biographies Texts Journals Research reports Histories	Globes Maps Morse code Photographs Fine art Music sheets Political records Cartoons Ballots	Building models Making clothes from patterns Reconstructing human culture from artifacts	Nonfiction books Biographies History Poetry Anthropology Geography Political Science Economics Human Relations	Family documents Letters Government documents Reports of interviews
Science	Weather Science editor Science news	Encyclopedias Texts Journals Histories Logs	Graphs Chemical symbols Films Thermometers Scales	Experiments Cooking recipes Computer printout	Biographies Physical science Natural science Nonfiction Poetry	Conservation records Notes of original scientific records Prescriptions
Mathematics	Business news Want ads Stockmarket reports Financial section	Technical journals Histories	Films Formulas Expanded notations Scales Number systems	Solving problems Computation	Biographies Nonfiction Poetry	Written problems Business ledgers
Literature	Book, play, and movie reviews Narratives in magazines	Bibliographies Biographies Texts Histories	Text illustrations Format (book, play, script) Music Works of art	Theme and plot analysis	Fiction Poetry Nonfiction	Creative writing by students in class
Art Education	Reviews	Histories	Picture books	How-to books	Biographies	Works of art Crafts
Music and Dance	Reviews	Histories	Records Dance steps Films	Dance steps Instrument directions	Biographies	Demonstrations
Drama	Reviews	Histories	Films Records Mime		Biographies	Plays

Adapted from Y. Goodman and C. Burke. *Reading Miscue Inventory Manual*, 1970.

Context for Learning 5

The importance of providing scaffolds, both for students who participate in the reading and writing process and for the teachers providing instruction (initially using unfamiliar strategies and processes) is fundamental [to the implementation of this guide.]
—Adapted from Raphael

Introduction

Context refers to the physical setting for learning, the classroom environment, the task set by the teacher or the learner, and the expected outcome of the task, whether it be a test, writing assignment, discussion, or activity. Only recently have researchers discovered the impact of context upon learning and the ways teachers can alter the context to improve student performance (Raphael, 1987).

Physical Setting

Walk into any content-area classroom and look around. Immediately, one can sense the atmosphere for learning. Are the students seated in even rows facing a teacher who is lecturing or leading a class discussion? Or are students seated in a circle, in small groups, or in pairs ? Are students working independently, reading, writing, or filling in worksheets? Or are they interacting? Is student work on display around the room? Above all, are students actively engaged in learning or passively taking in information?

Now, imagine you are a student who must walk into this classroom five days a week, 180 days a year. And consider that each day, students enter seven or eight different classrooms, each with its own special learning environment. What kind of learning takes place in those classrooms? How is learning in one different from learning in the others? Researchers estimate it takes five to ten minutes at the start of each class for students to adapt to different teaching styles and subject matters and to prepare themselves to use the thinking patterns associated with each content area (Pavlik and Piercey, 1989).

Classroom Environment

The classroom environment is a major context for learning and has a significant impact on student achievement. Students are more likely to succeed if teachers believe that virtually all students can master the basic processes of learning and if teachers structure an environment in which they gradually release the responsibility for learning to students.

Risk-Free Environment

When learning is viewed as a competitive activity and students measure success by how well they are doing compared to other students, they become more concerned about avoiding failure and embarrassment than about learning. Students learn best in an environment in which they feel free to make hypotheses and test them out. To foster such an environment teachers must focus on supporting and extending learning rather than controlling it. Students should feel free to share opinions, comments, and reactions. Differing opinions should be valued and treated with respect. Information processing rather than information receiving should be the major activity. Negotiation and collaboration among students and between students and teachers should occur. Teachers should draw out and focus students' ideas and reinforce and support risk-taking behaviors.

Grouping/Cooperative Learning

Grouping practices have enormous implications for the learning environment. The current practice of either having students work as individuals competing against the performance of a classmate or working in ability groups does not create an environment conducive to learning. Many low-performing students will never reach the top of their class no matter how hard they try. Because they have such a small chance for success, they either give up or become disruptive. High achievers, on the other hand, may not do their best because they are not being challenged, and they know they will be near the top even if they do what is for them mediocre work.

Learning is greatly influenced by classroom interactions.

An alternative to competition in the content-area classroom is cooperative learning. In a classroom emphasizing cooperative learning, students in small, heterogeneous groups help each other succeed while working toward a common goal. Classwide projects require a number of different talents that use the strengths of all students.

Through peer tutoring and reciprocal teaching, students act as teachers as well as students, and thereby monitor someone else's learning in addition to their own. And conversations among students in which they assert, defend, and question their thinking help them learn from one another.

According to Johnson and Johnson (1987), students who interact cooperatively achieve more, are more positive about school and themselves as learners, and are more effective personally.

Task

Task refers to assigned materials, purposes for instruction, and students' understanding of a lesson's objectives. Instructions such as

"Read pages 92 to 108 and answer the questions at the end" give students no direction for reading. As a result, students either plod through assigned readings with no purpose except to finish, or they don't read the material at all knowing that the teacher will lead a discussion in which they will be told the important points. When they are forced to respond to questions or study guides, students rely on what Pavlik and Piercey (1989) term "ping pong" reading. They look first at the question (ping) and then scan the text for the answer (pong), going back and forth without really reading. In effective classrooms, teachers state the task and its goals, how the task fits in with previous learning, and why it is important.

Gradual Release of Responsibility

Content-area teachers often complain that teaching students how to learn takes too much time. However, time spent teaching the important strategies for learning in a discipline can have a tremendous impact on students' ability to learn independently in the future.

Figure 2 illustrates the characteristics of instruction that move students toward independent use of strategies. According to this model, students develop the ability to apply strategies to become independent learners through instruction that gradually shifts the responsibility for initiating the use of a strategy from the teacher to the student.

During the first stage of instruction, content-area teachers direct the use of a strategy. They describe the strategy students will be learning and tell students how and where they should employ it (Duffy and Roehler, 1986). This "all-teacher" stage often takes the form of direct instruction and/or modeling by teachers.

After learning a strategy under teacher direction, students need to implement it on their own with content materials. Allowing students to practice while providing feedback on how they are doing is a more powerful teaching method than presenting many examples. During this guided practice stage, teachers must create an environment that is both motivating and encouraging. Students should interact with each other cooperatively, and teachers should provide additional instruction and modeling as needed. Teachers adjust their level of support to the difficulty of the material and the task and remove support gradually as students show increased proficiency with a strategy. Eventually, students should be able to use a strategy effectively and selectively in a variety of reading situations. At this point, students are in control of their own learning.

While strategic instruction emphasizes helping students manage cognitive processes, the effect on motivation cannot be overlooked. Students' expectations regarding success and failure are derived from previous learning experiences. Students who experience repeated failure in the classroom often see themselves as helpless. Strategic teaching can alter students' beliefs about themselves by providing them with a new set of experiences in which they have succeeded through their own efforts (Jones, Palincsar, Ogle, and Carr, 1987).

Figure 2

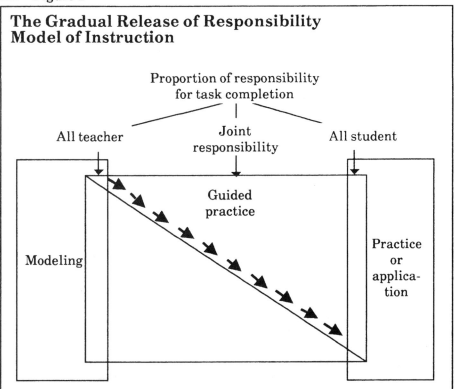

The Gradual Release of Responsibility Model of Instruction

Proportion of responsibility
for task completion

All teacher   Joint
responsibility   All student

Guided
practice

Modeling

Practice
or
applica-
tion

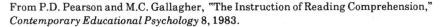

From P.D. Pearson and M.C. Gallagher, "The Instruction of Reading Comprehension," *Contemporary Educational Psychology* 8, 1983.

Outcome

Students who read for real purposes know why they are reading and how they will use the information. When teachers rely on such devices as "pop quizzes" to see if students have read assigned material, they reinforce the idea that learning is a meaningless game.

Assessment of learning in a strategic classroom is less a matter of how much students learn and more an assessment of how well they are able to use the information they have learned in discussions and through writing. The interactive model of reading describes learning as the construction of meaning. During this process new information is connected with what students already know and a conceptual change takes place. How can we measure that change? How do we see that the student has thrown out misconceptions and filled in sketchy or inadequate background knowledge? Pop quizzes and multiple-choice tests cannot measure real learning. Discussions, on the other hand, help students formulate and refine new knowledge and try out ideas.

Writing

Writing is one of the most powerful techniques for helping students learn and think critically about content information. A number of writing formats are included in this guide. Each of these strategies is designed to enable students to think about and restructure what they have learned and to use new knowledge to solve problems. Summaries, for example, are a good way for students to say what they have learned in their own words (*A Guide to Curriculum Planning in Reading*, p. 158). Problem/solution and opinion/proof are formats related to frames that help students recognize organizational patterns used by authors and reorganize information in their own minds. RAFT and other creative writing formats encourage students to see subjects from different perspectives.

Influence of Context

Because emphasis has now shifted to active, independent, strategic learning and teaching, this guide presents a challenge to teachers to create new classroom environments. Learning does indeed involve knowing certain strategies, but more than anything, it involves knowing when to use strategies and, to put it simply, wanting to use them. Teachers need to consider a variety of contexts for facilitating this kind of learning in content-area classrooms so that students can gradually take control of their own learning, and teachers can concentrate on helping students master the important concepts of their discipline.

The Strategic Teacher 6

The instructional model presented in this guide along with the corresponding strategies and supportive research all suggest that we are on the brink of helping all students learn how to learn.

Introduction

How can teachers of social studies, science, mathematics, foreign language, or any other content field provide instruction that is consistent with the Wisconsin Model of Reading Comprehension? How can they incorporate into their teaching what is known about learners, texts, and the context of learning to foster strategic learning behaviors? The answer lies in first examining what it is that teachers actually want their students to learn.

The primary goals of classroom teachers is to teach students how to organize and integrate important concepts and information as well as to become more independent in their learning. Teachers do not expect students to learn everything they will ever need to know about a subject area before graduation from high school. Rather, they want to cultivate life-long learners, mature readers who can meet the learning demands of their careers and their personal lives (*A Guide to Curriculum Planning in Reading*, 1986, pp. 16-17).

Content-area teachers make decisions both as subject matter specialists and as instructional leaders (Smith, 1986). This dual role has a number of implications for strategic teaching. First, it requires teachers to be thinkers and decision makers. Strategic teachers spend a great deal of time thinking about what they are doing and why they are doing it. They consciously decide what to teach and how to teach it, and they use text materials to implement those decisions (*A Guide to Curriculum Planning in Reading*, 1986, pp. 83-89).

Second, this dual role assumes that teachers operate from a rich knowledge base and clearly understand how that knowledge is delivered to their students through various organizational patterns in texts. Moreover, they understand how students learn and which teaching/learning strategies are most effective for their field.

And third, this dual instructional role highlights the responsibility of the teacher as a model and mediator. Strategic teachers demonstrate the thinking processes that go into effective learning. Through modeling and coaching, they help students internalize these behaviors and become independent learners (Jones, Palincsar, Ogle, and Carr, 1987).

Figure 3 shows the steps involved in strategic instructional planning. It guides teachers through a series of decisions that take into account content-area teachers' dual role as subject matter specialist and instructional leader.

The Teacher as a Subject-Matter Specialist

Strategic selection of appropriate content is especially important because many textbooks fail to adequately differentiate between important and relatively unimportant facts and information.

As subject-matter specialists, strategic teachers identify what is important for students to learn based on what students already know. Strategic teachers then determine what needs to be done to link students' prior knowledge with new content.

To do this, strategic teachers examine textbooks and supplementary material and decide which information is central to the learning of important concepts, what vocabulary must be understood, and what the objectives will be for each lesson. Thus, teachers approach texts as decision makers, ready to use what is appropriate and ready to discard the rest. This contrasts sharply with the notion of teachers as followers who adhere to teacher's guides, teaching all material merely because it appears in the book.

Strategic teachers emphasize cognitive processing and awareness rather than rote memory and accurate answers.

Strategic teachers also examine the organizational patterns of texts and plan ways to help students use frames to learn targeted material.

Finally, strategic teachers determine the purpose for learning. This purpose, which might be retention of facts, assimilation of new knowledge, or restructuring of knowledge, determines the task for a lesson. The task, in turn, defines the most effective learning strategies. During a lesson, strategic teachers evaluate how well students apply learning strategies. After a lesson, they assess whether or not students have integrated and can apply new knowledge (*A Guide to Curriculum Planning in Reading*, p. 141; Jones, Palincsar, Ogle, and Carr, 1987).

The Teacher as an Instructional Leader

As instructional leaders, strategic teachers are concerned with how students approach learning as well as what they actually learn. This role demands a careful evaluation of both teaching strategies and learning strategies.

Teaching strategies are the techniques teachers employ to help students learn content. Teaching strategies are selected to prepare students for reading, to guide students in their learning of the content during reading, and to enhance or build upon the content after reading (Blanton and Moorman, 1987; Herber and Nelson-Herber, 1987). When used effectively, teaching strategies develop independent learning skills. Ultimately, the responsibility for learning should shift from the teacher to the student.

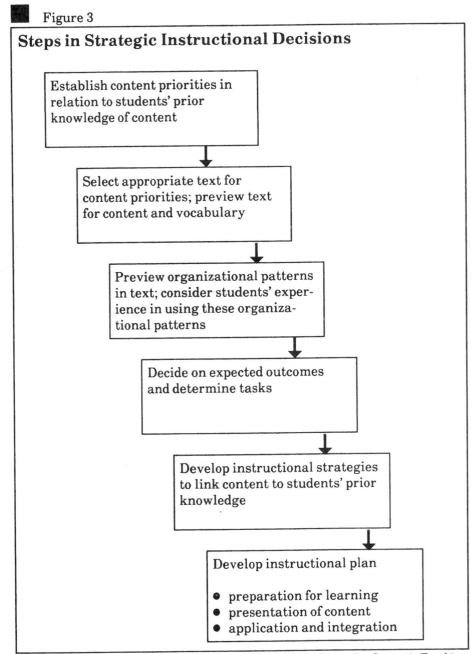

Figure 3

Steps in Strategic Instructional Decisions

Establish content priorities in relation to students' prior knowledge of content

Select appropriate text for content priorities; preview text for content and vocabulary

Preview organizational patterns in text; consider students' experience in using these organizational patterns

Decide on expected outcomes and determine tasks

Develop instructional strategies to link content to students' prior knowledge

Develop instructional plan

- preparation for learning
- presentation of content
- application and integration

Adapted from B.F. Jones, A.S. Palincsar, D.S. Ogle, and E.G. Carr, eds. *Strategic Teaching and Learning: Cognitive Instruction in the Content Areas*, 1987.

Learning strategies refer to behaviors initiated by students before, during, and after reading. These strategies are often referred to as "study skills." That term, however, has a rather limited connotation. Study skills are generally associated with specific techniques such as notetaking and surveying or with general behaviors such as concentration and time management. Missing from most discussions of study skills is the *thinking behind the learning*—the metacognitive, self-directed aspects of learning. Moreover, teachers tend to think of these skills as abilities that once learned are automatically used in all learning situations.

In contrast, learning strategies emphasize cognitive processes. For example, a specific system of notetaking will not in itself guarantee student learning. What students need to do to make notetaking successful is to internalize the cognitive processes involved in selecting and organizing information. If students merely write what they read or hear, without selecting what is important and organizing it in some meaningful manner, then the format in which the notes have been written is immaterial.

Learning strategies enable students to become independent learners. But they are not skills students simply learn in a single lesson. They must be taught and modeled within the context of each subject area over an extended period of time (Jones, Palincsar, Ogle, and Carr, 1987). They must be taught as a means for learning content, not as ends in themselves.

Obviously, it is artificial to separate effective teaching strategies from learning strategies. Both attempt to elicit the same cognitive and meta-cognitive behavior from students. In this guide, strategies will be referred to as teaching/learning strategies. Successful teaching/learning strategies enable students to activate background knowledge, focus learning, select and organize appropriate information, and integrate new information with prior knowledge. Effective teachers describe strategies, show students why they are appropriate, and teach students how, where and when to use them. Good instruction leads students to internalize strategies so that they can apply them during self-directed phases of learning.

Strategic teachers select teaching/learning strategies according to the specific content to be learned, the text organizational patterns, the level of learning desired, and the characteristics of learners.

A Model for Strategic Teaching

Figure 4 presents a framework for incorporating strategic teaching into instructional decision making. The framework divides strategic teaching into three phases: preparation for learning, which takes place before reading; presentation of content, which takes place during reading; and integration and application, which takes place after reading. The corresponding student phases of strategic learning are analyzing/planning, monitoring/regulating, and reflecting (*A Guide to Curriculum Planning in Reading*, p. 22). The framework identifies both the strategic teaching tasks and the corresponding student thinking processes for each phase. Effective teaching/learning strategies for each phase are highlighted.

Preparation for Learning

During this phase, teachers encourage students to analyze the task at hand and plan an effective approach for learning content. The cognitive processes involved are activating appropriate background knowledge and focusing learning (Blanton and Moorman, 1987; Jones, Palincsar, Ogle, and Carr, 1987).

Teachers determine core concepts and information and select appropriate text for presenting them. They prompt students to activate and assess what they already know about this content and note any misconceptions students may have. Then, if necessary, teachers employ a teaching/learning strategy that will help give students necessary background information. KWL Plus and PReP are teaching/learning strategies that assess and activate background knowledge.

Teachers preview the text with students so students see how it is organized and guide the selection of appropriate learning strategies.

Finally, strategic teachers establish clear purposes for reading the material, focus student interest on the content, and explain the task.

Presentation of Content

Strategic teachers are more active during this phase than is often suggested. Rather than merely supervising silent reading or answering questions about content, strategic teachers help students think about what they are reading and model strategies for accomplishing the assigned task. Teaching/learning strategies, such as graphic outlines and organizers, help accomplish these goals.

Teachers help students use text frames to select and organize important information. They encourage students to compare what they are reading with what they already know about the subject and with what they predicted about the content while previewing the material. This helps students recognize gaps in their knowledge and contradictions between what they know and what is presented.

Teachers guide students to ask questions about what they are reading and to monitor how well they are understanding the text. Teachers also coach students to withhold judgment on what they are reading, encouraging them instead to think "I don't really know what this is about yet" or "I'm not sure yet if my predictions about this are correct or not." Modeling of these metacognitive processes through teacher "think alouds" is an especially effective strategy during this phase of instruction.

Integration and Application

During this phase, teachers help students integrate new information with existing knowledge and apply what they learned. Students reflect on what they read and decide whether they achieved the purpose, fulfilled the assigned tasks, and remembered the information.

Strategic teachers reinforce use of organizational patterns to restructure and integrate new information. They help students confront and correct misconceptions. And they encourage students to apply new knowledge to increasingly complex and diverse situations and tasks such as writing exercises, discussions, role playing, and research projects.

Writing exercises, such as summaries, RAFT, and position statements, are especially effective teaching/learning strategies for the integration and application phase of instruction. Writing, an essential component of content learning, is integral to many of the teaching/learning strategies outlined in this guide.

Figure 4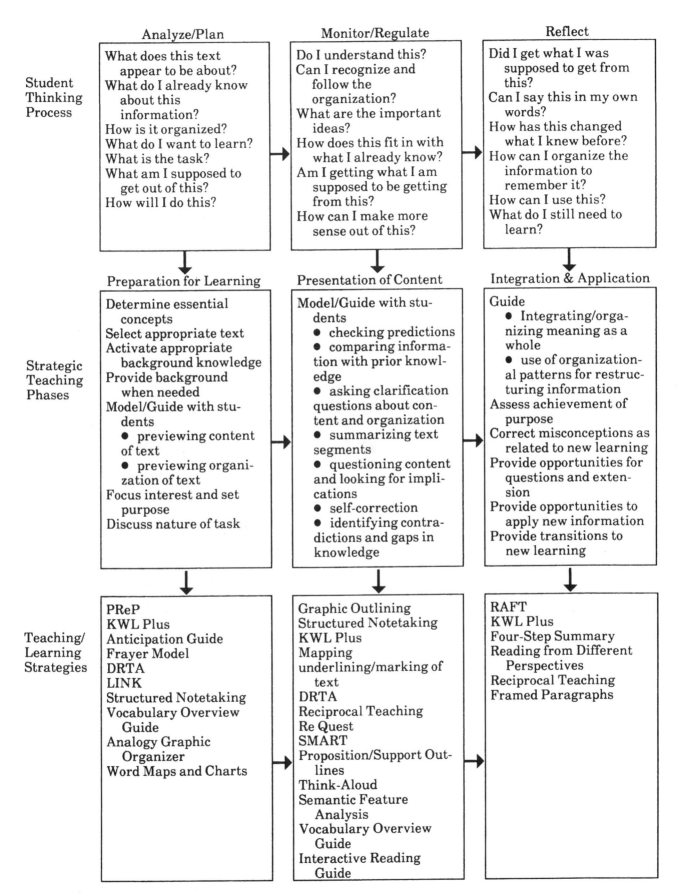

A Model for Strategic Teaching and Learning

	Analyze/Plan	Monitor/Regulate	Reflect
Student Thinking Process	What does this text appear to be about? What do I already know about this information? How is it organized? What do I want to learn? What is the task? What am I supposed to get out of this? How will I do this?	Do I understand this? Can I recognize and follow the organization? What are the important ideas? How does this fit in with what I already know? Am I getting what I am supposed to be getting from this? How can I make more sense out of this?	Did I get what I was supposed to get from this? Can I say this in my own words? How has this changed what I knew before? How can I organize the information to remember it? How can I use this? What do I still need to learn?
	Preparation for Learning	Presentation of Content	Integration & Application
Strategic Teaching Phases	Determine essential concepts Select appropriate text Activate appropriate background knowledge Provide background when needed Model/Guide with students • previewing content of text • previewing organization of text Focus interest and set purpose Discuss nature of task	Model/Guide with students • checking predictions • comparing information with prior knowledge • asking clarification questions about content and organization • summarizing text segments • questioning content and looking for implications • self-correction • identifying contradictions and gaps in knowledge	Guide • Integrating/organizing meaning as a whole • use of organizational patterns for restructuring information Assess achievement of purpose Correct misconceptions as related to new learning Provide opportunities for questions and extension Provide opportunities to apply new information Provide transitions to new learning
Teaching/ Learning Strategies	PReP KWL Plus Anticipation Guide Frayer Model DRTA LINK Structured Notetaking Vocabulary Overview Guide Analogy Graphic Organizer Word Maps and Charts	Graphic Outlining Structured Notetaking KWL Plus Mapping underlining/marking of text DRTA Reciprocal Teaching Re Quest SMART Proposition/Support Outlines Think-Aloud Semantic Feature Analysis Vocabulary Overview Guide Interactive Reading Guide	RAFT KWL Plus Four-Step Summary Reading from Different Perspectives Reciprocal Teaching Framed Paragraphs

Implementing the Guide: Staff Development

7

Gone are the days when delivering a "teacher proof" box of new curricula was accepted as the way to produce immediate change.
–Hall

Introduction

This guide was written to help reading specialists, administrators, and teachers apply specific examples of cognitive instruction to content-area reading. However, to make the contents of this publication a reality, systematic, long-term program of staff development is needed for significant changes in teacher behavior to take place—changes that preclude students' development of strategic learning (Alverman, Moore, and Conley, 1987; Vacca, 1981; Cole, 1979).

Research indicates that change in teacher behavior does not come with the usual workshop. School staff are continually being challenged to move beyond the "good time" inservice day typically offered to designing staff development workshops that support change (Hall and Hord, 1988). Increasing emphasis is placed on phased and content-specific workshops to support the change process as it occurs.

One type of inservice, information transmission, uses lectures and discussions to present a new approach and the theory or research behind it. This type of inservice is the most common—and the most unpopular (Alverman, Moore, and Conley, 1987).

A second type of inservice, skill acquisition, is designed to strengthen old skills or learn new ones. Results from this kind of staff development indicate that it does not bring about change in teachers' classroom behavior. The development of a strategy does not ensure its use in the classroom.

The third and most effective type of inservice, behavior change, includes sessions similar to the above but is designed with a commitment to changing teacher behavior through peer coaching. Peer coaching teams teachers who then work together as they study new skills, polish old ones, and implement changes in the classroom. This type is the only model that provides a reasonable chance of changing teaching practices. Showers (1984) confirmed that coaching is key to the effective transfer of learned behaviors from the workshop to the classroom. However, coaching, without the study of theory, observation of models, and opportunity for practice and feedback, will falter.

This guide offers two plans of staff development for implementing its contents. School staff are encouraged to experiment with various time and staff arrangements. Both plans reflect a collaborative professional growth model where reflection and experimentation are encouraged in a supportive environment. They also highlight the reading specialist as the key person for making the staff development meaningful.

The Short-Term Plan for Staff Development, on page 57, suggests an approach to helping groups of content-area teachers gain familiarity with the guide and learn some new strategies for practicing in the classroom. This model could be repeated for different groups of content-area teachers within convenient blocks of time.

The Long-Term Plan for Staff Development, developed for use with the Wisconsin Rural Reading Improvement Project, describes a program aimed at the entire school or school district staff over three to five years. This plan involves more study and understanding of strategic learning by reading specialists, administrators, and content-area teachers. There is also more collaboration among teachers practicing strategies over an extended period of time in different settings and providing support for each other.

Role of Administrator/Principal

The support of school administrators and principals is essential to the success of a staff development program for strategic learning processes. Administrators should understand that implementing a model for strategic learning will take three to five years. They can provide the necessary incentives, support, budget, and time teachers need to transform the contents of this guide into a meaningful curriculum. Principals play an important role in offering encouragement and support for teachers taking risks by using new strategies and for teachers involved in peer coaching and action research. Supportive climates are necessary in order for the success of each activity. The principal plays a key role in establishing and maintaining those climates.

The critical aspect of this leadership role is in the exercise of day-to-day actions that are required to initiate and sustain the change and improvement process.

Role of Reading Specialist

The reading specialist plays a key role in implementing a content-area reading program. First, the reading specialist must become a learner by studying the theoretical base or rationale of strategic learning or by observing demonstrations of persons adept in using the strategies by practicing them and by developing a level of expertise. The reading specialist can then serve as the school or district expert who provides demonstrations for teachers. The contents of this guide suggest a radical change in the way most teachers instruct students in how to learn from text. Simply knowing the steps of a particular strategy without understanding why or how they work does not guarantee use or success. Teachers must be able to help students change a strategy when it doesn't work and must modify their instruction to meet the needs of specific students. Teachers should also understand why a strategy works in cognitive theory. Then, they are able to teach strategies in more meaningful ways to ensure that students apply the strategies independently and appropriately.

Teach students strategies for learning from text in meaningful context.

In order to develop expertise, reading specialists may need to collaborate with other reading specialists, attend conferences, and investigate other avenues to help them understand the theory, discuss the meaning, and obtain feedback.

This self-as-learner step is useful for the reading specialists' primary role and leadership responsibility—which is to serve as a resource to content-area teachers, introducing them to the guide and the research, and helping adapt the contents to their specific subject areas. The most difficult task for the reading specialist will be getting teachers to relate to new information and then transferring that information into their curriculum. Serving as a resource for fellow teachers may be a different role for some reading specialists; many are not trained to work with other teachers this way. The Wisconsin Department of Public Instruction encourages the training of reading specialists to include collaboration with other teachers in classroom action research.

Reading specialists also must demonstrate enthusiasm for implementation of the strategic learning ideas, relate well with other staff, provide assistance and ideas for implementation, and be willing to serve in a supporting advisory capacity to teachers who must alter classroom behavior. They must feel comfortable and competent modeling strategies for other teachers. Initially, they may want to model strategies before a few content-area teachers who are receptive to new ideas. These teachers should be recognized as leaders by their fellow teachers. Later, the specialists must support the development and use of peer coaching teams, action research, and informal assessments of students' strategic learning in varying content areas.

Role of Content-Area Teachers

The heart of staff development is the content-area teachers. A program will not be successful if the teachers themselves are not enthusiastic and responsive.

Change is a process, not an event.
–Hall

Since human attitudes change from the inside rather than from the outside, we gain insights that lead to behavioral change only when we perceive a need for such change within ourselves. Recognizing the need for change does not come easily for many content-area teachers. Rather, it comes as a result of considerable uneasiness, confusion, and perhaps pain resulting from the recognition that present methods aren't working well. Teachers might think, "My students aren't able to learn from the textbook."

We hope this guide will nudge content-area teachers to consider their role in developing strategic learners and will make them comfortable teaching the strategies. We also hope this guide will eliminate the impression that content-area teachers must become *reading* specialists. Because they are *content* specialists, however, they become the models and experts for showing students how to learn from content and texts.

This guide is a staff development tool—not a teacher-proof programmed curriculum package. Staff development should occur to achieve implementation of the contents as well as to help individual teachers experience change and growth.

   I.   Provide background
- A. Need for strategic learning
- B. Research supporting strategic learning
- C. Participant involvement recognizing need for strategic learning in their content area

  II.   Describe strategies used in strategic learning
- A. Provide model for instruction
- B. Provide detailed description and demonstration of each step of process
- C. Provide model lessons for different content areas

 III.   Demonstrate individual strategies
- A. Model process (what, when, why, how)
- B. Transform strategy for classroom use
- C. Plan for implementation

 IV.   Implementation of strategy
- A. Teachers identify which strategy they would like to try
- B. Teacher and reading specialist collaboratively implement strategy

  V.   Demonstrate and implement peer coaching teams
- A. Develop coaching teams
- B. Learn how to provide appropriate feedback

 VI.   Feedback from implementation (coaching)
- A. Reading specialist and content-area teacher discuss strategy and process
- B. Examine strengths and weaknesses
- C. Plan refinement
- D. Plan for next use of the strategy combined with coaching

VII.   Further implementation
- A. Reading specialist supports content-area teacher demonstrating strategy for other teachers
- B. Participants use reading specialist and content-area teachers as support and coach (peer coaching)

Adapted from L.J. McClain-Ruelle, "Finessing Reading Strategies into the Secondary Content Classroom – An Inservice Delivery Model," *Reading Improvement* 25, 1988.

Long-Term Plan for Staff Development

Reading specialists should develop their own expertise in strategic learning in the content areas and staff development in terms of peer coaching, action research, and longitudinal views of change. It would be best if reading specialists found a peer and/or colleague with whom they can co-learn and co-develop their expertise.

- Study the theory of strategic learning by reading this guide and selected readings. Discuss readings with peers and colleague, and with an expert when possible.
- Attend meetings, view videotapes, or visit classrooms of expert teachers in order to observe persons relatively expert in strategic learning. Follow with discussions when possible.
- Practice strategic learning instruction many times and in controlled conditions. Obtain technical feedback from a knowledgeable person and/ or a colleague who is a co-learner.
- Study the dimensions of staff development—peer coaching, action research, and longitudinal change. Discuss when possible.
- Observe demonstrations by persons experienced in peer coaching, attend reporting sessions of teachers who have conducted action research projects and others who have participated in long-term staff development projects. Examine the roles and responsibilities of administrators in such projects.
- Practice peer coaching. Get technical feedback when possible.
- Plan an action research project. Get technical feedback when possible.

With district and school administrators and selected content-area teachers, plan a long-term (three- to five-year) staff development project for strategic learning in the content areas.

- Provide administrators and teachers the theoretical base for strategic learning, peer coaching, action research, and long-term staff development.
- Demonstrate model lessons for different content areas. Begin with demonstrations by an expert (on videotapes, for instance), or experienced teachers. Follow demonstrations with discussions that focus on and review theory related to strategic learning.
- Visit classrooms of more experienced teachers.
- Demonstrate peer coaching. Discuss the role of the principal in establishing and promoting the experimental and sheltered environment needed for successful peer coaching.
- Illustrate action research projects and the environment needed to support them.
- Plan classroom demonstrations to initiate peer coaching. Develop a rapport with classroom teachers, pointing out what to observe, predicting successes and pitfalls, and discussing the results.

- Encourage teachers to demonstrate strategic teaching and learning to their peers. Followed by discussions.

  Develop initial implementation plans.

- Assign peer coaching teams.
- Plan classroom demonstrations by teachers with lessons where it appears the strategy will be most productive and likely to succeed. Repeat practice and feedback sessions.
- Reread parts of original readings, read new material, repeat demonstrations by more experienced teachers, and review theory with an expert.
- Design action research projects with interested and motivated teachers.
- Invite the principal to observe the new methods. The goal is to help the administrator understand the new classroom environment and conditions related to strategic learning and peer coaching.
- Develop and use informal assessment procedures for evaluation.

  Plan for extended implementation.

- Forecast transfer problems through an all-day trail in an actual classroom.
- Support teachers as they shift from old programs to ones that exemplify strategic learning.
- Encourage teachers to develop a long-term plan that accounts for possible student resistance to the new approach.
- Maintain the plans with rereading, repeated classrooms visits, and reviews of theory.

Like athletes, teachers will put newly learned skills to use—if they are coached.
—Joyce, Showers

Adapted from the Wisconsin Rural Reading Improvement Project.

The Content Areas

8

*The idea that reading instruction and
subject matter instruction should be
integrated is an old one in education, but
there is little indication that such integration
occurs often in practice.*
–Becoming a Nation of Readers

Introduction

Although strategic learning involves concerns across content areas, each subject has its own characteristics. In this chapter the subject area sections are organized around the Wisconsin Model for Reading Comprehension, which focuses on reader considerations, text characteristics, the context for learning, and teacher considerations (*A Guide to Curriculum Planning in Reading*, pp. 10-14). Model lessons also are included for health, literature, mathematics, science, and social studies. The health, science, social studies, and mathematics lessons are divided into the three teaching phases described in Chapter 6 (preparation for learning, presentation of content, and integration and application). The literature lesson focuses on integrating the phases and is a generic model for analyzing character traits. Strategies suggested here are described in more detail in Chapter 9.

Art serves a number of objectives: perceptual awareness, creativity, aesthetics, understanding culture, communication skills, and understanding one's self. Art education aims to foster and promote the qualities of conceptual understanding, aesthetics, creative behavior, craftsmanship, understanding the content of art, and understanding one's self. For an explanation of these goals, see *A Guide to Curriculum Planning in Art Education*, published by the Wisconsin Department of Public Instruction.

Learner Considerations

Art education includes the following areas: aesthetics, art history and criticism, and art making. Success in the subject requires the ability to work with and integrate knowledge in each of these areas.

Much of art involves appraising and understanding visual forms. Students must appreciate aesthetics, which is necessarily ambiguous and subjective. Because of aesthetics' broad definition, many students may experience frustration.

Art history stresses the field's roots. Students need to know the background behind artists' approaches to expression, art's relation to society as a whole, and their response to art. Students often lack sufficient background in art and in history to understand art heritage.

Art criticism requires students to understand and then judge works of art. Students must learn about the factors related to form and content, such as composition, medium, and function. Students often lack background knowledge about form and function. In addition, students often have had little practice in making critical judgments.

Art making requires students to read instructional and procedural material, so-called reading-to-do. Since much of school reading requires "reading to learn," students likely will have had little experience with reading to do. Readings associated with art making often involve basic procedures that can be altered in a variety of ways. As a result, students must not simply follow step-by-step instruction, they must perceive the overall goal of the process.

Art vocabulary presents unique problems. Students may not know the specific and technical vocabulary used in the art classroom. General words such as "form" and "line" have very specific, yet unusual, meanings in art.

Text Characteristics

Art-related reading may use a variety of text structures. Art history typically follows a chronological or thematic structure. Reading related to techniques uses a sequential structure. Understanding art criticism requires knowledge of a text structure that in turn depends upon a knowledge of art forms, art techniques, and schools of art. Art forms present different reading demands. For example, students may be required to "read" a painting and must, therefore, understand how aesthetic scanning might be used.

Readings found in popular media and in text materials in other subject areas, require students to recognize art in a variety of materials from newspapers and popular magazines to high-quality publications.

Context

Learning in art, often thought of as activity-oriented where students draw, paint, and sculpt, is increasingly using more written materials. As a result, students have to learn to integrate the knowledge from hands-on activity with the knowledge that they gain from reading.

Art classrooms vary from the regular elementary classroom to a self-contained art classroom. Within the different rooms, students have different access to art materials.

Art classes consist of students with a wide range of abilities. At times, the classes offered an alternative for the academically less able, and reading was kept to a minimum.

Teacher Considerations

Art teachers need to help students take a problem-solving approach to art. Rather than viewing art as a set of steps, students should see art as a creative response to a problem. Teachers must help students develop backgrounds in aesthetics, art history, and art criticism, and students must be able to integrate their understanding of these areas.

Art teachers must increasingly use written materials in their curricula. The material should include art history and criticism and contemporary stories about art found in newspapers and magazines.

Foreign language education focuses on a number of areas: increasing global interdependence and cultural diversity, improving learning skills and career education, and helping students gain a number of personal benefits. To understand the full picture, see *A Guide to Curriculum Planning in Foreign Language*, published by the Wisconsin Department of Public Instruction.

Learner Considerations

Learning in foreign languages involves four major skill areas: listening, speaking, reading, and writing. Learning in foreign languages resembles learning in the language arts.

The content of foreign language involves learning the language, learning the culture, and learning to learn.

Learning the language centers on reading and speaking. Students must learn the skills and rules of oral understanding, speaking, writing, syntax, and grammar. They also must adjust to both unfamiliar vocabulary and unfamiliar sentence structures.

Learning the culture requires exposure to customs, music, art, and other aspects of the societies that speak the language. Students must understand how cultures differ and build a background of experiences related to the culture associated with the new language.

Learning to learn in the new language suggests that students use the language skills to help them continue to learn. For example, students must read for global meaning rather than just translating a passage. In many ways, learning a foreign language mirrors the initial learning of English.

However, foreign language vocabularies consist of words that usually do not have English equivalents. When they do use cognates, students must distinguish true and false ones. Students often don't have the advantage of being able to recognize a word when they hear it spoken.

Text Characteristics

Foreign languages present unusual syntax. As word order differs from that in English, students must learn to understand the different patterns and ultimately to acquire a new set of syntactic expectations.

Some foreign languages also present orthographic patterns that are quite different from English. Like syntax, the conventions, such as spelling and capitalization, may be different from those in the English language. Students, therefore, need to learn a new set of patterns.

Beginning-level texts, often quite different from other content-area texts, use consistent lesson formats where words are introduced through systematic practice. While these lessons can help students, they bear little resemblance to other content-area texts or to actual foreign language text structures.

Foreign language readers with limited vocabularies face the same problems as English readers with limited vocabularies. The vocabularies may not help students prepare for actual reading and speaking situations in the foreign language because the limitations create artificial situations. As a result, students need to bridge the gap from foreign language textbooks to real foreign language situations.

Context

Foreign language classrooms, typically English-speaking environments, limit the opportunity to practice. In addition, the available practice happens in somewhat unnatural settings. To become proficient in a foreign language, students need situations to practice in a larger context. Learning expands when students encounter situations where they are encouraged to speak and think in the new language. Travel abroad is encouraged. Language immersion situations, partial and total, also encourage students to use the new language.

The contexts for foreign language vary widely from district to district. As a result, program emphasis varies from total immersion to a stress on grammar.

Teacher Considerations

Teachers must understand that learning foreign language resembles primary reading. Students must "decode" new words and use these words for communication and comprehension.

One factor affecting a student's ability to comprehend and remember, prior knowledge, establishes a student's success to relate the new to the known to build a new knowledge base. The teacher should consider initially using content that conceptually will be quite familiar to the students. When helping students learn words, use cognates to build on the students' prior knowledge.

As students learn new concepts, they will need support strategies, and teachers must model metacognitive processes that will help students approach foreign language study.

Health education should teach and reinforce the skills, attitudes, and practices necessary for a healthy lifestyle. Educators must emphasize health as a value in life and encourage critical thinking, decision-making, and problem-solving skills regarding health. For elucidation on these points, see *A Guide to Curriculum Planning in Health Education*, published by the Wisconsin Department of Public Instruction.

Learner Considerations

The health education curriculum attempts to influence student's attitudes and appreciation for the importance of good health. It also attempts to build inquiry skills that explain and analyze health-related problems and concerns. If the content is presented in a purely didactic fashion, students may resist the material. Much of the reading material—designed to develop knowledge of facts, terminology, concepts, generalizations, and principles—helps students focus on the importance of health. If students simply memorize the facts and terminology, they may find health education very difficult and irrelevant to their lives.

A focus on developing skills that aim to maintain or improve health will motivate students to take personal responsibility for their own well-being. Application of these skills must be reinforced outside of the classroom for students to see relevance to daily living.

While students usually have background knowledge and experiences for many of the topics, they also have misinformation and misconceptions about these topics.

Text Characteristics

Textbooks, just one information source, should augment various other health-related materials, including magazine articles, pamphlets, brochures, computer information, and newspapers. These different materials require different reading strategies.

Health education texts often revolve around such topics as nutrition, personal health, and growth and development. These topics appear in the curriculum each year. As students progress through the health curriculum, textbooks treat topics with increasing detail and abstraction.

These texts, usually organized in a concept/definition, compare/contrast, or problem/solution patterns, often use a personal active voice that addresses the student as "you" and encourages student involvement. Health textbooks contain numerous graphics to illustrate their content. Students may encounter problems with these graphics unless they learn to read them. Vocabulary tends toward the technical and scientific. Chapters often resemble biology texts in both content and format. As a result, students may have problems learning from health texts without instruction and background.

Context

Instructional material in health lends itself to a variety of approaches, most activity-oriented. Assignments should focus on activities that encourage students to make decisions in sample situations, applying the knowledge from their text. Audiovisual materials, such as films, videotapes, and physical models, are often used to illustrate concepts. Class reports and discussions often emerge from group activities.

Although health can be taught in a number of ways, imparting real-life meaning is essential. While students may be asked to define vocabulary at a literal level, eventually they must apply those concepts to real-life situations. Students should develop personal meanings so that they learn the skills, concepts, and information from the course.

Teacher Considerations

A Guide to Curriculum Planning in Health Education suggests that learning strategies necessary to developing positive health behaviors should assist in problem-solving and decision-making skills. Students must develop a means of inquiry and the ability to think critically.

Model Lesson: Wellness

Concept

Wellness means total good health, not just the absence of sickness. Wellness means being the best you can be physically, intellectually, emotionally, and socially. Suggested material for this lesson: "Well, Well, Well with Slim Goodbody," a video series with accompanying readings. The series of 15 15-minute episodes was produced by Wisconsin Public Television, Madison, and was designed for grades 1 through 3.

Preparation for Learning

Procedure

1. The teacher leads a discussion of wellness by reviewing what students have learned and by eliciting the students' personal experiences with wellness.
2. During the discussion, the teacher categorizes students' responses around these major categories: physical, intellectual, emotional, and social; the teacher guides students to use these categories.
3. The teacher notes any misconceptions that students may have regarding this topic—some students, for example, may believe that having a handicap means being unwell.
4. The teacher motivates students with an activity that increases their awareness of wellness. The teacher leads a discussion of the meaning of a sound mind in a healthy body, or introduces the topic through a problem/solution frame that requires students to find solutions to a health problem and to consider the consequences of each solution they propose. These solutions could be reconsidered after reading the text and viewing the videotape.
5. The teacher previews the text with students, noting the text structure. The teacher explains any graphic aids so students will be able to learn from them.
6. The teacher provides a conceptual frame in the form of an outline of a spider map (Example 1), filling in major concepts presented in the text.

Example 1

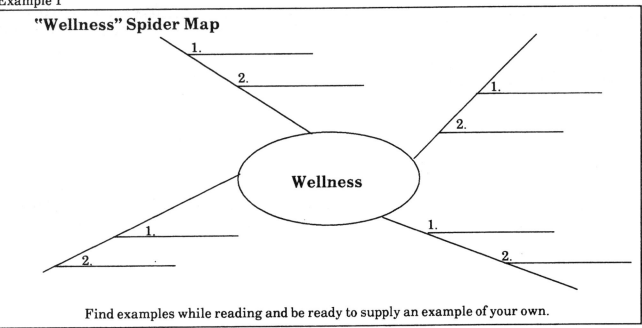

"Wellness" Spider Map

1. _____
2. _____

1. _____
2. _____

Wellness

1. _____
2. _____

1. _____
2. _____

Find examples while reading and be ready to supply an example of your own.

7. The teacher introduces vocabulary relating to the key concepts, such as choice, habit, and responsibility. The teacher asks students the category the word belongs in and the factors that distinguish it from other words and lists some examples of the concept (see Example 2).

Example 2

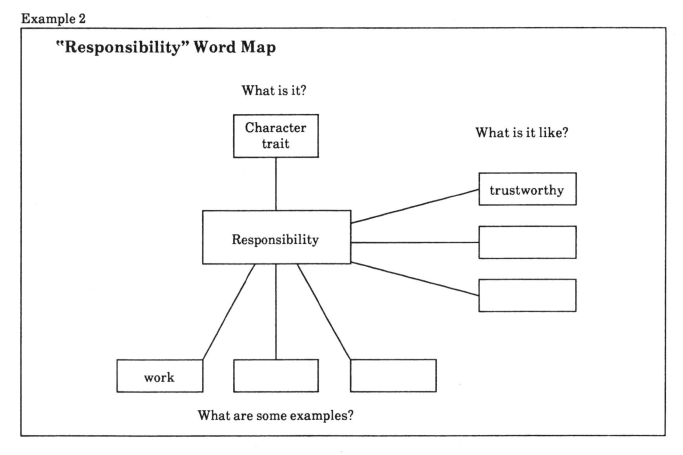

"Responsibility" Word Map

What is it?

Character trait

What is it like?

trustworthy

Responsibility

work

What are some examples?

8. Direct discussion toward a purpose. "What do I want to know?" "What do I have?" "What would I like to learn in my reading?" These are a sample of the questions that will likely arise during the lesson.

Presentation of Content

Students can use a spider map as a guide for reading and for taking notes, filling in supporting details and examples. Students could read and discuss the reading in a partner situation.

Integration and Application

Students can use the spider map frame for writing activities that summarize the chapter. The frame also can be the basis for follow-up discussion—"What did we learn?" "What do we need to find from other sources?"

Health concepts can be integrated into the entire curriculum by using a thematic approach. *A Guide to Curriculum Planning in Reading* (pp. 119-120) suggests some general guidelines for developing thematic units. Example 3 suggests a thematic approach for integrating wellness across the curriculum.

Example 3

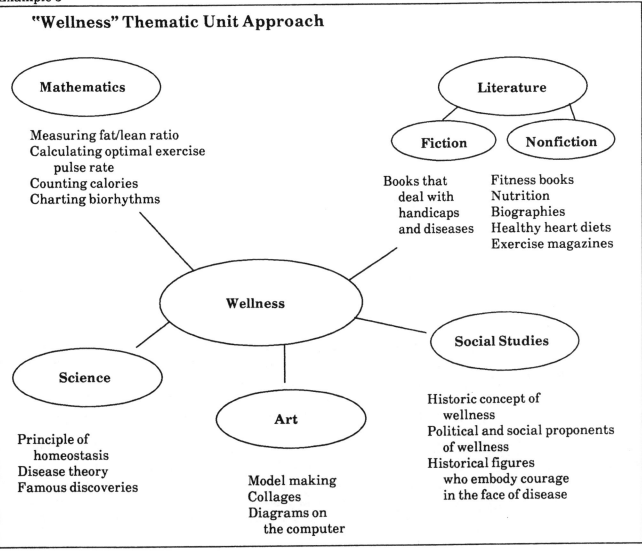

"Wellness" Thematic Unit Approach

Mathematics

Measuring fat/lean ratio
Calculating optimal exercise
   pulse rate
Counting calories
Charting biorhythms

Literature

Fiction

Books that
   deal with
   handicaps
   and diseases

Nonfiction

Fitness books
Nutrition
Biographies
Healthy heart diets
Exercise magazines

Wellness

Social Studies

Historic concept of
   wellness
Political and social proponents
   of wellness
Historical figures
   who embody courage
   in the face of disease

Science

Principle of
   homeostasis
Disease theory
Famous discoveries

Art

Model making
Collages
Diagrams on
   the computer

The Learner in Literature

A quality K-12 literature program should: teach literary forms and conventions that enable students to recognize, analyze, interpret, and evaluate literary works; foster oral and written language skills; expand personal and social understanding and appreciation; and help develop a lifelong habit of reading. The learner can become intrinsically motivated to explore, to develop competence, and to become a more confident, able thinker, reader, speaker, and writer. Consult *A Guide to Curriculum Planning in English Language Arts*, published by the Wisconsin Department of Public Instruction, for detailed goals and recommended organization of the subject.

Learner Considerations

Literature instruction has emphasized numerous approaches that put the text at the center of literary analysis. Recently, however, literature educators and reading researchers have restored the student as the key element in the creation of a literary work (Department of Public Instruction, 1986). The reader is not passive, but an active, dynamic learner interacting with the text to create the literary work.

Because the learner must bridge the gap between known and new knowledge, the learner's background and experience is as important as the content itself. By integrating the new information, students can use schemata to help them understand the content. By comparing a character's actions in one novel to those in another novel, students can identify the motives behind the actions. They also need to recognize the difference between their world and the world portrayed in the text. Students may encounter social, cultural, and economic perspectives totally different from their own. When that happens, students with misconceptions or inadequate background knowledge may struggle to identify, infer, or react to the author's intentions and the characters themselves. Limited knowledge may spawn difficulties with literary devices such as irony, satire, figurative language, and allusion. Literature is complex, abstract, and open to multiple interpretations, and comprehension depends on the students' experience reading literature and their level of cognitive development.

The ability to interpret literature is another vital factor for students. Asking them to write an essay interpreting the theme of a selection may cause some students to simply stare at a sheet of paper. They do not know where to begin because they do not understand the process that went into the writing. Giving readers a set of questions—"What is the setting?" "Who is the main character?" "What is the problem?"—may not help students achieve any coherent interpretation of the selection. While students may be able to answer basic questions, the questions can fragment their perceptions about the text. Many students need guided response activities or scaffolding instruction to generate an interpretation.

Text Characteristics

With fiction, the student may encounter a complex interaction of characters, plots, settings, and narrative structures that hinder analysis. With poetry, inverted syntax, poetic patterns, and compressed ideas can pose problems. Drama requires student inferences based on careful attention to dialogue, body language, stage directions, and settings. Nonfiction, such as essays, biographies, and documentaries, may be difficult because of unfamiliar writing patterns.

Literary writing follows many patterns, and patterns found in its content include story, grammar, theme, and characterization. Some patterns may highlight key words and phrases that cue the reader. When students see the signal words "in contrast," they can predict the pattern of compare/contrast. These markers are often omitted in more sophisticated text, and students must infer the pattern.

Students benefit from prior knowledge about forms and patterns. They need to learn how to preview, identify, and use text structures and story grammar to aid comprehension. The text structures and frames described in Chapter 4 will help students focus attention on important structural elements and direct their thinking to a logical plan. (A K-12 scope and sequence for developing understanding of text structures in both narrative and expository text can be found in *A Guide to Curriculum Planning in Reading*.)

Context

Imagine a classroom where students are assigned to "read pages 243 through 274 in the anthology and answer the questions at the end of the selection." Many students would read just enough to answer the questions. These students superficially scan the material, while others may not read at all. In this situation, students have no clear understanding of their task.

Since students have read narrative text before entering middle and high school, teachers assume that students can analyze a task and set their own purposes for reading. Teachers should not make these assumptions. Students need a range of response strategies, namely identifying, describing, connecting, interpreting, and evaluating. Effective teachers help students to develop purposes, identify goals and outcomes, recognize connections to previous learning, and explain the importance of the task.

Effective instruction provides an environment with many opportunities for student interaction. Literature teachers often have students work cooperatively in large groups using a particular strategy such as brainstorming; they also may have students in smaller groups using other strategies.

Questioning, another important activity, incorporates strategies that encourage students to generate questions before, during, and after reading to help them interact with the text and learn more effectively. Effective literature classrooms foster creativity by promoting an atmosphere that is open and free, where students can take risks and mutual respect is evident.

Teacher Considerations

Literature teachers need a strategic approach to vocabulary instruction. Effective instructional strategies provide opportunity for in-depth analysis, word associations, and extensive vocabulary use. Direct vocabulary instruction that involves brainstorming and categorizing is critical. This instruction will help students link new information to prior knowledge and relate to literary elements.

Instructors need to teach effective comprehension strategies for reading, writing, discussing, and listening. These strategies include summarizing, representing text graphically, using organizational patterns, elaborating, relating to prior knowledge, and paraphrasing. Through these, students will enhance their understanding, appreciation, and enjoyment of literature.

The teacher must foster students' perceptions of literary works by ordering and organizing images, ideas, and emotions related to the text. These elements come to life through students' prior knowledge of life and language and create a self-awareness in relation to the text.

Since some students respond on a very elementary level or have difficulty generating responses, teachers need to provide systematic and explicit instruction to help students articulate their responses. Jones (in Harris and Cooper, 1985, pp. 105-130) refers to this as response instruction, which involves teaching students how to structure their answers to cover the desired content, use the appropriate text structure, and give the intended response. Students need to analyze questions for the information they provide and require. Text structure should be stated or implied in the questions that direct student thought.

Teachers need to help students organize their thinking by using frames and graphic outlines. The model lesson shows how matrix outlining and analysis can be used to help students analyze and respond to literature by describing and comparing character traits. The matrix outlining encourages a written response to literature. Students should generate numerous high-level generalizations and organize information to reflect the text's structure.

Model Lesson: Character Traits

Concept

What techniques did the author use to reveal the character traits of the main character? Compare and contrast characters one and two with regard to character traits.

In this lesson the teacher guides students through the use of two frames, description and compare/contrast, to pull out material essential to understanding the text.

Procedure

1. The teacher reviews the concept of character traits and discusses the difference between moods, character traits, and facts about a character.
2. The teacher writes on the chalkboard in matrix form the names of the characters who will be compared and contrasted.
3. The teacher lists the traits for each character (Example 1).

Example 1*

Pablo	José	Mary
brave	cowardly	honest
gloomy	cheerful	brave
impatient	friendly	cheerful
loving	mean	friendly
suspicious	irresponsible	neat
responsible	destructive	patient
self-reliant	bragging	modest
		loving

4. The teacher discusses how each was revealed (author's statement, metaphor, dialogue, character's action) and writes them in a matrix (Example 2).

Example 2*

Character	Action	Reason	Trait
Dan	He leaves his pen.	He wants the detective to be misled.	tricky cunning
the detective	He sees the pen and assumes Dan is trying to be misleading.	He assumes that the witnesses will try to trick him.	smart alert

5. The teacher reviews the signal words for compare/contrast paragraphs (see Chapter 4).
6. The teacher models the writing of both compare/contrast and descriptive paragraphs that use the information from the matrices, and includes the components listed in Example 3, then guides students as they do the same.

*From Harris, T., and E. Cooper. *Reading, Thinking, and Concept Development*, 1985, pp. 122, 123, 125.

7. In small groups, students share their paragraphs and critique each other's for completeness, making sure all the elements listed in Example 3 are contained.

Example 3

Characteristics of Compare/Contrast and Descriptive Paragraphs	
Compare/Contrast	Descriptive
The compare/contrast paragraph, which describes the similarities and differences between two characters, should contain the following: ● an introductory sentence identifying the characters and title ● a general statement, summarizing how the characters are similar and/or different ● a more specific, but still general, statement telling how the characters are similar ● details supporting the generalization regarding similarities ● a second general statement stating how characters are different ● details supporting the generalization regarding differences	The descriptive paragraph should contain the following: ● a topic sentence stating the character's name, book title, and trait ● details showing how the trait was revealed ● a description of the character's actions, the character's dialogue or thoughts or a statement by the author.

Mathematics instruction should seek to develop the students' ability to solve problems. Students need a sound knowledge and understanding of mathematical skills and concepts in number and numeration, measurement, geometry, algebra, statistics, discrete mathematics, and problem solving. The concepts should be taught not as isolated bits of knowledge, but as tools for solving realistic problems. By integrating these concepts, mathematical problem solving moves students into the realm of higher-order thinking. For a full explanation of these goals, see *A Guide to Curriculum Planning in Mathematics*, published by the Wisconsin Department of Public Instruction.

Learner Considerations

Mathematics' content can pose many difficulties for the novice learner who sees the subject as abstract. The use of concrete or semi-concrete examples in the form of pictures or illustrations transforms mathematical ideas to a less symbolic, hence less abstract, form.

Mathematics teachers frequently ask students to memorize abstract definitions and rules. However, before they reach this level, students need concrete experience. Children entering school know how to count and how to represent problems with objects. They know how to manipulate objects to form a collection of items that represents the answer to the posed problem, and this is how they learn mathematics. As they acquire experience, they acquire the power to generalize from their experience. Mathematical symbols become useful, and students recognize that hundreds of situations can be represented by $6 + (\ \ ) = 13$.

Mathematical symbolism $(-, \div, \rightarrow)$ and mathematical vocabulary rarely venture outside the classroom. The absence reduces opportunities to use them and increases the need for reminders during mathematics instruction. Further, the vocabulary should be introduced only after the concept is understood. Students need extensive experience with commutative relationships before the property itself is understood, for example. "Commutative" can then be introduced as a name for the examples. Another potential problem, ordinary words with specific meanings in mathematics—"factor," "similar," "equivalent," and "divide"—should be explained so students don't confuse the ordinary meanings with the mathematical meanings.

A term's definition will expand as a student's level of understanding becomes more sophisticated. For instance, multiplication of whole numbers may mean repeated addition, but multiplication of integers means something different. Teachers need to make students comfortable with the idea that some terms have precise meanings and others are more tentative ones to be modified as skills develop. As students move from one level to another, they return to the same concepts but with new meanings.

Many students have difficulty solving story problems. Teachers frequently expect that computational skills apply to problem-solving skills, but that is not so. While problem-solving difficulties may be equated with reading difficulties, often students who can read very well cannot conceptualize a problem in terms of an action and carry out the action to arrive at a result, nor can they accurately express the relationship using mathematical symbols. The student may not have made the connection between actions and their mathematical representations. The teacher may have tried to teach problem solving through a key-word approach. The student may be unwilling to persevere due to a misconception that mathematical problems can be solved quickly or not at all.

The content in mathematics often leads to misconceptions, some carried over from the real world and some from experience with formal mathematics. In formal mathematics, research has shown that mistakes consistently made by students stem from misapplications or generalizations of procedures. For example, children working a subtraction problem may think, "Always subtract the smaller number from the larger," (Lindquist, 1987, pp. 125-127) thus arriving at the following conclusion: $486 - 128 = 362$.

Text Characteristics

Several factors make learning from a math textbook difficult. The text is primarily graphic rather than verbal. The prose is compact and requires slow, deliberate reading to comprehend the concepts. Most children never learn to read mathematics text; teachers generally assume that students will not read the instructional portion and use the textbook as a source of practice exercises.

Mathematics-related material lacks the structure found in materials from other disciplines. Paragraphs often lack topic sentences, or they may be so compact that every sentence seems to be a topic sentence. In addition, the vocabulary is very technical and not part of the common vocabulary of students at that grade level.

A further problem, illustrated in the following diagram, is the variety of eye movements required to read mathematics.

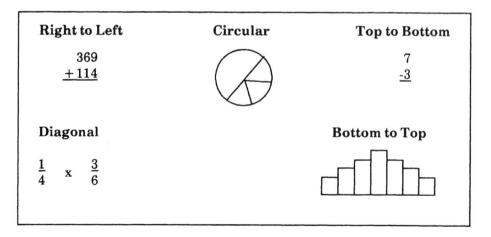

Context

Teaching mathematics frequently takes the form of stating a mathematical principle, illustrating the principle with a few examples, and asking the children to practice similar examples. This form of instruction prevails at all grade levels.

First-grade teachers of mathematics often teach as though students have no prior knowledge and learn by imitating an example. However most children already know a considerable amount of mathematics when they start school. The knowledge enables students to solve a variety of problems, even though they do not know how to add and subtract. Despite this, teachers emphasize number facts and computational algorithms, introduced with the expectation that these skills will teach problem solving. As a result, student ability to solve problems actually declines, probably because the new structures either conflict with or have no connection to those already known by the students.

For most, the utility of mathematics arises from applications and problem solving related to citizenship and careers. Computational skills not applicable in life situations have little, if any, value. All mathematics should be taught in the context of problem solving and applications.

Applications of mathematics in other domains, such as social studies, science, business, and vocational education, should be emphasized. Students will have difficulty making connections between related mathematical ideas unless teachers help to make these connections apparent.

Teacher Considerations

When developing an instructional plan, the teacher must address monitoring and self-evaluation. In mathematics, as in other disciplines, the teacher needs to bring forward the student's prior knowledge and address any misconceptions. Mathematics should apply to the student's life by having instruction organized around extensive problem modeling situations. Instruction should progress from concrete models to pictorial representations but should return to the concrete each time a new concept is introduced.

Many content-area strategies illustrated in this guide work well in mathematics. Particularly useful are strategies that address vocabulary and strategies that help students see a process from beginning to end, such as Think-Alouds and DRTA.

Teachers should try to incorporate the following in their mathematics instruction:

- classroom environments where problem solving can flourish
- materials and texts that prepare students for flexible, deep, and broad problem-solving ability
- problem-solving strategies at all grade levels
- manipulative materials and illustrations throughout the elementary and middle grades
- explicit problem-solving models

- discussion about the processes used in solving problems
- observation of student interaction for insight to their construction of mathematical processes and structures
- heterogeneous collaborative student groups to solve problems
- emphasis of the applications of mathematics to other disciplines and relationships among mathematical ideas
- development of concepts before introduction of vocabulary and symbolism
- text materials in reading lessons and explicit instruction in how to read mathematics
- student practice only after understanding has been achieved

Model Lesson: Rhombus Concept

When students learn a new concept in mathematics, it is particularly important to include a review of prior knowledge. Studies show that students taught how to solve one type of problem may not be able to solve problems parallel in structure (Lindquist, 1987, pp. 125-127).

This model is sequential on paper but recursive in practice. Teachers who work through a concept with students can identify and rectify misconceptions and help students integrate new information with prior knowledge.

Preparation for Learning

Procedure

1. The teacher assesses how much students already know. Generally, students are familiar with parallelograms, rectangles, squares, and their properties.
2. The teacher tells students the goal of the lesson: they will add one quadrilateral, the rhombus, to their knowledge of polygons.
3. The teacher activates background knowledge by having students list the properties they know about squares, rectangles, and parallelograms (see Example 1).
4. The teacher keeps students focused on the task by providing hints or examples.

Example 1

Quadrilaterals				
Questions	**Rhombus**	**Square**	**Rectangle**	**Parallelogram**
What is it?		A square is a rectangle with 4 ≅ sides	A parallelogram with right angles	A quadrilateral with 2 pairs of ∥ sides
What does it look like?			←square	
What properties?		4 sides ≅ 4 rt ∢s 2 pairs ∥ sides	opp sides ≅ 4 rt ∢s 2 pairs ∥ sides	opp sides ≅ opp ∢s ≅
Diagonals?		d are ≅ d are ⊥ d bisect each other	d are ≅	d bisect each other
Line symmetry?		4 lines	2 lines	none in
Perimeter?		add the sides $s+s+s+s=4s$	add the sides $l+w+l+w$	same as rectangle
Area?		$A=bh$	$A=bh$	$A=bh$
Rotational symmetry?		90° 180° 270° 360°	180° 360°	180° 360°

Adapted from M. M. Lindquist, "Strategic Teaching in Mathematics," in *Strategic Teaching and Learning*, 1987.

Presentation of Content

Procedure

1. The teacher shows sketches of different kinds of polygons (Example 2).

   Example 2

   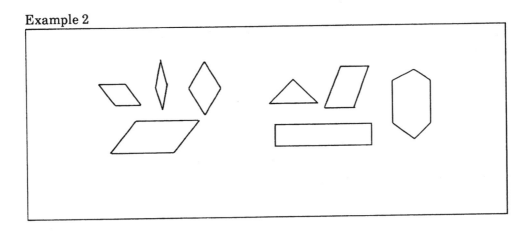

2. Students examine and discuss examples and nonexamples of rhombuses. After asking students what characterizes a rhombus, the teacher helps students develop a definition. The teacher guides students toward the understanding that all squares are rhombuses, but not the converse.

3. Once students understand what a rhombus is, the teacher places students in small groups and instructs them to investigate the properties of a rhombus, particularly symmetry, perimeter, diagonals, and area. The teacher asks each group to draw four different rhombuses and answer questions such as the following:

   - Do all rhombuses have diagonals of equal length?
   - Do any rhombuses have diagonals of equal length?
   - How many lines of symmetry does a rhombus have?
   - If you cut a rhombus on its diagonal what do you find?
   - How do you determine the area of rhombus?

4. The teacher guides students toward the assimilation of ideas by having the groups report how they arrived at their findings. The class discusses any questions that arose during students' investigations.

Integration and Application

Procedure

1. The teacher helps students understand that all squares are both rhombuses and rectangles and that all three are parallelograms. The following graphic organizers may help.

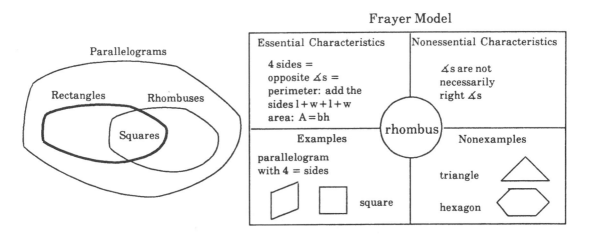

2. The teacher assesses what students have learned by discussing old misconceptions. With some children, the teacher may want to extend the concept of a rhombus by using other examples, such as trapezoids and kites (Lindquist, 1987, pp. 125-127).

All students should encounter music—through performance by ear and by reading music, through discussions of music and its materials, and through composing music in new and interesting ways—to develop to their fullest potential. The student in music encounters and works with music in a variety of ways and at different cognitive levels. These levels and the subject's goals are described in *A Guide to Curriculum Planning in Music Education*, published by the Wisconsin Department of Public Instruction.

Learner Considerations

Learning in music involves three modes: performing, describing, and creating. In performance, students perceive and understand aural cues and visual symbols that signal student response. In description, students use abstract thinking to discuss music they have read about, heard, or performed. In creation, students analyze, synthesize, and evaluate as they decide what musical materials to use, how to use them, and whether the use was successful.

Learning music is similar to learning language. Both depend on the student's ability to perceive similarities and differences in sounds, shapes, and symbols. In music, several symbol systems operate simultaneously. For example, when performing the student must respond to such factors as notation, time signatures, and aural and visual cues.

Often the reading in music is very abstract. Music history and criticism refer to sounds, but students usually cannot read and listen at the same time. Consequently, students often lack concrete experience with the works referred to in music texts.

Since much of music is both written and aural, students must understand the relationship between what is on the page and what they hear or play. Students must be prepared for these translations.

Performance in music requires experiential reading, a type of reading-to-do. Since most school reading is reading-to-learn, students may have little experience with the other. Reading music also involves a basic procedure like reading notations, where interpretation is as important as, if not more important than, the original procedure. As a result, students must not simply read the notes, but must have an idea of the whole process.

Text Characteristics

Different types of music-related reading use different types of text structure. Music appreciation, like history, typically employs a chronological structure, a thematic structure, or a comparison structure.

Musical notation has certain patterns; text structure in music often refers to the type of composition to be studied or performed. Within these compositions, musical phrases or notational sequences often repeat, and students must learn to expect and recognize these structures and patterns.

Reading notation presents particular problems since music's structure revolves around syntax quite different from that of English. Instead of subject-verb-object structures, students deal with notational structures governed by an unfamiliar set of rules.

Vocabulary in music is often specialized, commonly using foreign words. Students often lack the vocabulary and may have difficulty pronouncing the words. Common words used in unusual ways also present special problems in music. Words such as "line," "note," and "tone" have specialized meanings. Students may not understand the word or recognize its significance in a music-related context.

Context

Learning in music is primarily an experiential hands-on activity that requires students to read-to-do. But students often lack the formal instruction to apply reading strategies in these situations.

Because of students' wide range of abilities, the teacher must accommodate diverse learning abilities as well as diverse music abilities. Moreover, music requires that students use their reading and musical abilities at the same time.

Teacher Considerations

Teachers must help students learn music's vocabulary to facilitate reading-to-do. The vocabulary should be taught in the context of the composition to be studied or performed and introduced before the lesson.

Music teachers should recognize that students may have problems reading music, not because of reading difficulties, but because of a limited background in music. Students may also have trouble reading music history because they have heard few of the musical works referred to in the history. Teachers should help students build their musical backgrounds to help them more effectively read about music. Teachers also must help students use background knowledge effectively by having students recall what they know before they read or perform.

Teachers should introduce more written materials in the music curriculum. This material should include history, criticism, and music-related writing in newspapers and popular magazines.

Music teachers can help students see the need for reading strategies in their classes. By helping students work with different types of text, teachers can help students understand the structures found in music and its writings. They must encourage students to see the relationships within the content presented. For example, they should help students see the patterns repeated in musical notation. Students can then develop expectations and predictions about music's materials.

The Learner in Physical Education

Physical education is unique in that it achieves educational objectives primarily through physical activity. Wherever possible, physical education should be coordinated with other fields and courses that have similar interests. Besides physical skills, students learn the basic principles of exercise, movement, health, and the cognitive components of sports, games, aquatics, and dance. Consult *A Guide to Curriculum Planning in Physical Education*, published by the Wisconsin Department of Public Instruction, for a more detailed description.

Learner Considerations

Because of physical education's unique approach, students and sometimes teachers may not consider cognitive learning as important. Students prefer doing to learning and are sometimes confused by written and verbal directions. But they need to know the "why" as well as the "how" of a skill or activity.

Students often fail to connect the benefits of learning physical skills and activities to lifetime pursuits such as recreation, nutrition, and health. Students need to understand how a specific activity can relate to others they might pursue after graduation.

Although most students possess adequate background knowledge for physical activities, they often have misconceptions and may jump to conclusions that could inhibit learning or even place students in danger. Students who are already familiar with sandlot baseball or televised football, for example, may not heed the directions or rules for these activities in class, thus endangering their own and others' safety.

Text Characteristics

Texts used in physical education classes tend to be handouts explaining rules or procedures that use step-by-step or sequential formats. Students are sometimes asked to read and interpret symbols and diagrams such as referee hand signals or play patterns. Other materials include sports and fitness magazines, the sports pages of the newspaper, and books and manuals. These materials can help students recognize the life-long benefits of physical activity, although time must be set aside for discussions, presentations, and reading.

Audiovisual materials and computer software are increasingly used in physical education to demonstrate activities or techniques. Students need to be taught how to use these to improve their own performance.

Context

The physical education classroom is an active atmosphere where learning takes place through doing. Feedback comes through teacher and student modeling, correction, and interaction. Students need a sense of the progressive development of physical skills and should not expect to perform perfectly the first time. Although students often compare themselves to classmates, the comparisons may be negative. Their effect can be minimized through a cooperative rather than a competitive classroom atmosphere where individual differences are appreciated.

Teacher Considerations

Physical education teachers need to determine which concepts to teach and the most effective means of teaching them. They should draw on the accumulated background knowledge of their students and help them see how new concepts relate to what they already know. When reading about a skill or sport is appropriate, written materials should be introduced to the physical education classroom.

Students need strategies for independently learning about different sports and activities, and teachers should incorporate these into their lessons. Teachers also need to model how new skills are learned and how existing skills are enhanced. Students also may benefit from learning how to visualize their own performance prior to participating in a physical activity.

Because of the increased use of audiovisual materials in physical education classes, students need instruction to work with these materials. After or during viewing, students should take notes or use study guides to comprehend the material.

The Learner in Science

Science has changed the way people think of the universe and has altered the process and quality of life. Specifically, science education includes four carefully integrated components: the nature of science, science knowledge, problem solving and the relationships among science, technology, and society. *A Guide to Curriculum Planning in Science*, published by the Wisconsin Department of Public Instruction, further explains these four aspects.

Learner Considerations

Nature of Science

The nature of science includes its historical development, its rules of operation, and its base of knowledge. Students need to approach science, as more than just a body of information, but rather as a process to understand the world and its environment.

Scientists often divide science into separate disciplines. While this practice helps them, the divisions have often "restricted the learning process because many science concepts and problems involve two, three, or more science disciplines" (Department of Public Instruction, p. 4).

While the integration of knowledge from science disciplines can aid learning, students also must learn the different processes and ways of thinking unique to each field. Students must balance both the integration and separation common to learning science.

Science Knowledge

Reading and learning in science provide new insights about the world. Students' natural curiosity, blended with text materials and learning experiences, build understandings of scientific concepts.

Learning in science depends heavily on background experiences. In order to understand and learn from what is read, observed, or experienced, students must have appropriate background knowledge. A potential problem, however, is that scientific knowledge often may be very different from student understandings about the world. These misconceptions can cause students to unknowingly resist new knowledge. Successful learning in science is really a process of conceptual change. Teachers and students should recognize both the positive and negative effects of background knowledge. While students must relate scientific theory and information to their own notions about the world, they also must recognize that some notions and ideas may be misconceptions that could prevent learning.

Scientific writing, often loaded with facts, concepts, and explanations, may force students to wrongly see science as a collection of facts and definitions and to become overwhelmed or defeated by the number of descriptive statements or new concepts. They may fail to distinguish main concepts from less important details because of the sheer volume of information or because of a poor organization of concepts. Graphic representations, however, will help the students to focus on main concepts and to clarify relationships.

Problem Solving

Problem solving is integral to successful learning in science, but many students have trouble thinking as scientists. Students need to understand that while science includes facts, rules, and definitions, science is best viewed as explanation that requires integration of the parts. Science learning should emphasize a problem-solving approach that focuses on how and why events happen. Students should adopt a problem-solving way of thinking as they learn to question, predict, and revise thinking.

Science, Technology, and Society

Students need to see the application of science in their lives. The interactions of science and technology with society illustrate how scientific knowledge can be applied to technology that produces goods and services used in society. Students should understand how these relationships can improve or harm our society. Opportunities for students to apply their new science knowledge and problem-solving skills to everyday issues should be numerous.

Text Characteristics

The characteristics of science textbooks may pose problems. Because published texts or teacher-made materials may include vivid descriptions or colorful photographs, the actual demands on the reader may appear to be deceptively simple. Students need to integrate the pictures and descriptions with their prior knowledge to completely understand.

As students try to distinguish main ideas from less important details, they may find too many new concepts on a single page or so many explanations or descriptions that they become confused.

Science materials use a variety of organizational patterns, from cause and effect to problem and solution. Graphic representations may help students recognize and understand relationships. Scientific writing often involves detailed explanation of complex processes and includes many compound and complex sentences as well as complex relationships between concepts. Further, it extensively uses boldface type, headings, and graphics to highlight important ideas. Students must learn to use these format aids carefully to distinguish important from less important information.

Like vocabularies in other subject areas, the vocabulary of science includes many new terms—many with Latin or Greek roots and many used in only one scientific discipline. Students might meet more than 20 new terms or concepts in one class period.

Context

Problem solving is vital in science. Students must learn to use strategies to solve real-world problems as well as classroom problems. They must learn to formulate hypotheses, test hypotheses, and question or alter hypotheses. Successful science students recognize that problem solving is crucial to learning scientific knowledge.

Field trips, guest speakers, projects, and activities reinforce understanding the relationship between scientific and technological concepts and society. Students who observe and participate in these activities will better comprehend written scientific information. They benefit from a context that includes activities with unexpected outcomes or conflicting results. Such activities motivate students and enhance problem solving skills. Students also must be able to work independently as well as cooperatively with other students.

Students are often curious about science as it relates to their personal world. The pace of science instruction must not be too fast; vast amounts of information and isolated facts may cause confusion and result in a loss of motivation.

Without intervention, many students may cling to unsuccessful strategies that limit learning because they do not lead to conceptual change. (Anderson, 1987; Roth, 1985) These unsuccessful strategies may include the following:

● Overdependence on prior knowledge—Students take information from their backgrounds rather than from the text to answer questions.
● Emphasis on isolated words—Students focus on isolated words or phrases and view science as random bits of information or terms to recall for the teacher and the test.
● Viewing learning as additive—Students do not relate text information to background knowledge and see science as a cumulative list of facts to memorize.
● Using prior knowledge to explain text—Although students attempt to use background knowledge, they assume that the text will verify and add details to what they know. The student says, "I already knew this." Text information is read but ignored, and misconceptions remain unchanged in spite of a strong ability to read.

Students need to be prepared for conceptual change. A successful learner understands that the text may lead to changes in thinking about the real world. This learner can spot confusing and conflicting text explanations. In addition, the learner will abandon misconceptions in order to resolve any conflicts.

Teacher Considerations

Activities and learning strategies that strengthen student background knowledge before reading and follow-up activities that promote application of knowledge after reading are both key components of student-centered instruction. Science instruction should provide students with adequate preparation before they read, guidance while they read, and direction for application of knowledge after they read.

Many science concepts are best taught in the laboratory through direct experiences. Teachers should help students learn to plan investigations and make observations independently. Teachers must understand and account for students' naive conceptions about the world. Otherwise, students will misinterpret or misunderstand new information. Students should discuss a new topic before activities begin so that their background knowledge links with the new content and any misconceptions become evident.

Teachers must systematically deal with student misconceptions and help students see that

● new scientific concepts may be in conflict with previous background knowledge;
● background knowledge may be inadequate, incomplete, or inconsistent with text information or evidence; and
● new conclusions and new understandings may provide better alternatives than preconceived notions.

Teachers must plan for this conceptual change by planning learning experiences that include a phase for preparation, presentation, and application/integration.

Discussions that focus on real issues help students relate learning in science to their personal world. Instruction that emphasizes the interactions of science and technology with society demonstrates new knowledge can lead to societal improvement.

Model Lesson: The Earth's Oceans

Concept and Materials

After learning about the earth's fresh water resources, seventh-grade students study the earth's oceans. A textbook provides each unit's base of information. Accompanying teacher activities provide laboratory experiences and student activities for review of main concepts.

Students have just completed a group experiment with fresh water and salt water. They observed that fresh water freezes, but salt water does not—at least not in the school's freezer. They also discovered that salt water sinks when added to a tank of fresh water.

Students are ready to read text passages about the properties of ocean water. The text includes an introductory paragraph and explains salt in ocean water, gases in ocean water, and temperature of ocean water.

Preparation for Learning

The LINK prereading strategy, which helps students relate background knowledge to new text information, provides a way for the teacher to evaluate background knowledge and introduce new concepts to students.

Procedure

1. The teacher puts the main concept, "ocean water," on an overhead.
2. Students list associations on paper. They are given two to three minutes to work independently or in pairs.
3. Responses are shared and listed. A list of associations might include:

Pacific	Whales	Cousteau	Shrimp
Salty	Octopus	Submarines	Tides
Deep			

Inquiries are made. Questions that emerge might be:

"I saw Salt Lake. Why do you float in Salt Lake?"
"Why did you put submarine there?"

4. Students discuss associations and question items. The purpose is to have students share and elaborate understandings. The teacher, remaining neutral, lets students discover errors or problems.
5. Students turn papers over. They have one minute to write what they know. The teacher also notes student knowledge, misconceptions, and limitations in background knowledge.

Presentation of Content

The teacher previews the text and decides on important information identifying helpful, complex, or misleading passages. The teacher also identifies the structure of the text information and matches that organization with a strategy to help students read for a specific purpose.

Example 1

"Properties of Ocean Water" Map

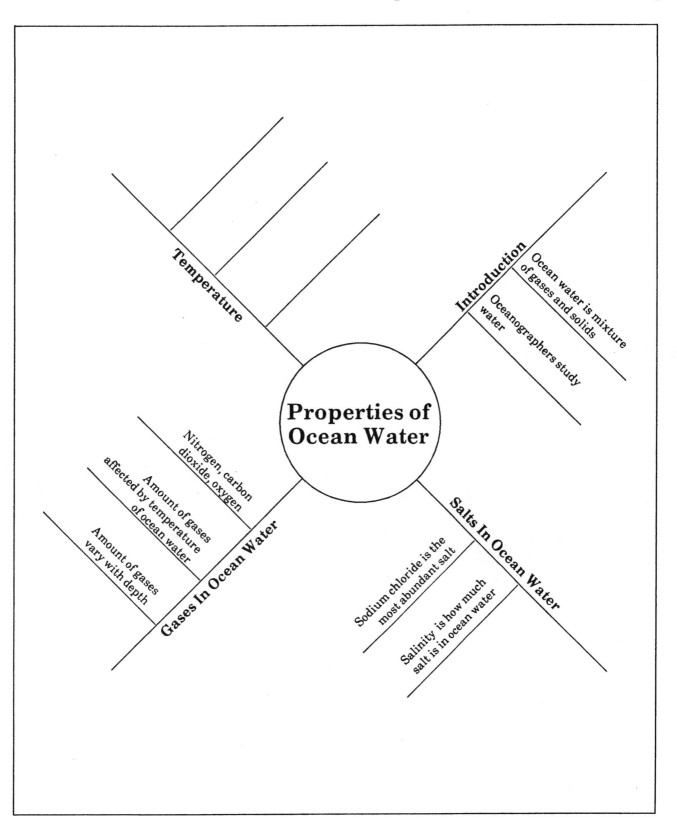

Temperature

Introduction
- Ocean water is mixture of gases and solids
- Oceanographers study water

Properties of Ocean Water

Gases In Ocean Water
- Nitrogen, carbon dioxide, oxygen
- Amount of gases affected by temperature of ocean water
- Amount of gases vary with depth

Salts In Ocean Water
- Sodium chloride is the most abundant salt
- Salinity is how much salt is in ocean water

A review of the text reveals that the properties of ocean water are described with separate headings for each property. The Mapping strategy will help students identify important details related to each property.

Students read and take notes using the mapping structure (Example 1). Although they recognize the map structure, the teacher leads students through the first two sections of the map to ensure that students understand the task and can identify key details. Students complete the map independently. Students may write phrases instead of complete sentences, but their notes should include only the most important information. When maps are completed, students work in pairs to check maps and share information.

Eventually, the entire class shares responses. The teacher notes key responses on the overhead and students may add or delete information. Students then compare their original prereading associations for the ocean water activity to new information. New information is added to the original association list and students delete any misconceptions. Students can use maps as they review text information and work in pairs to check knowledge of important information.

Integration and Application

The teacher recognizes that while students learned the basic properties of ocean water, they also need to recognize important cause-and-effect relationships often missed in the first reading. Students reread the text for a specific purpose: to locate and define cause-and-effect relationships between climate, animal life, sunlight, and ocean water.

The teacher guides a discussion of the text structure and points out a cause-effect relationship in a paragraph. Students then work in pairs to complete a cause-and-effect outline as they re-read specific parts of the text (Example 2).

The Four-Step Summary writing procedure is a strategy that can be used to reinforce or apply what students have learned.

Procedure

Students, in groups of three, complete summary preparations for the text. Students follow the following summary format:

1. Identify main concept.
2. Identify important subtopics related to main concept.
3. List important details to be included with each subtopic.
4. Write a summary statement that establishes the importance of the relationship between the subtopics and the main topic. This formula should be used to complete the following activity.

Students work individually to summarize the lesson. "You have just been hired as a guide at the Boston or Los Angeles aquarium. The museum wants you to introduce tourists from Wisconsin to the ocean exhibit. Your job is to explain to the tourists the important differences between the fresh water normally found in Wisconsin and the ocean water they see on the coast. Use the Four-Step Summary Outline to write one or more paragraphs to convince your boss that you know something about ocean water and can do your job. You will give the presentation to the tourists, who arrive tomorrow morning, so make sure that your paragraphs about ocean water are complete and interesting."

Example 2

Properties of Ocean Water

Cause $\longrightarrow$ **Effect**

Warm/hot climate _____

Salinity is greater _____

Little rainfall _____

Water evaporates, salt remains _____

Volcanic eruption _____

_____

Rivers and glaciers _____

_____

$\downarrow$

Summary Statement

Ocean water is salty because of volcanoes, glaciers, and rivers.

The Learner in Social Studies

Social studies instruction includes five goals: developing enlightened citizens; building an appreciation and understanding of our cultural heritage; promoting the acquisition of knowledge and skills; encouraging the joy of learning; and teaching how to learn. The student faces a challenge to use this education as the basis for a lifetime of understanding and participating in our democratic process. For an in-depth description of these goals, see *A Guide to Curriculum Planning in Social Studies*, published by the Wisconsin Department of Public Instruction.

Learner Considerations

Social studies emphasizes political, economic, and social decision making. The student must evaluate materials with a critical and inquiring mind. The student encounters three factors in the social studies classroom—*information*, isolated fragments of fact, which in themselves are not terribly useful; *knowledge*, structured information, which shows relationships between pieces of information; and *wisdom*, the use of information and knowledge, which leads to decisions and action on those decisions.

Much of the *knowledge* of the social studies centers on ideas and theories related to human behavior, both past and present. The student must relate the various pieces of *information* to the larger realm of human behavior—in history, psychology, sociology, geography, political science, or any of the other social sciences. However many students have difficulty making these connections.

Social studies researchers emphasize the importance of background knowledge for learning. Students who know little about the information presented in a social studies classroom will fail to understand many social science concepts. And because this information does not seem meaningful or useful, many students will lack the motivation to create a personal knowledge of the concepts studied.

Another potential problem, social studies concepts tend to be complex and abstract and often open to multiple interpretations. Students must draw from a broad background to fully grasp abstract concepts such as liberalism, imperialism, or culture. Many general vocabulary terms, such as "demand," "right," or "socialize," have different meanings in the social studies. These specific meanings can confuse students.

Text Characteristics

Robinson (1983) observed that the textbook remains the dominant source of information. Social studies materials, usually expository in style, increasingly use primary sources. Other materials and media are used often, but primarily as supplements to the textbook.

Social studies writing frequently follows a problem/solution frame. Other common frames or patterns of organization are goal, people, descriptive, compare/contrast, conflict/cooperation, and causal. Main ideas of paragraphs in social studies textbooks often are not clearly stated. Topic sentences of paragraphs frequently are not first sentences, or are omitted entirely.

Social studies readings sometimes fail to clearly explain major concepts. As a result, readers may have difficulty realizing the relations between various facts and important concepts or theories that help us gain insight into human behavior. In addition, students may come to regard learning from some textbooks as a "Trivial Pursuit" exercise (Department of Public Instruction, 1986, p. 7).

Graphics, especially important components of social studies materials, provide essential information in the form of maps, charts, tables, graphs, and pictures. But unless students learn to use graphic information, they may skip this key part during reading.

Context

Instruction usually centers on a single textbook, despite a wide range of reading abilities, interests, and backgrounds in a particular class. Lectures and teacher-led discussions of the content are frequent classroom activities.

Reading in the social studies generally follows a recitation model that requires students to answer questions based on a textbook reading. Questions typically target a literal level of understanding and focus on facts and figures.

Social studies teachers should increasingly focus on higher-level thinking skills through primary sources in textbooks that encourage development of critical thinking and evaluation. Discussion and small-group activities allow students to make judgments and defend positions by using information they encounter in reading. Independent assignments that require students to locate and examine materials on a designated topic place an important emphasis on research and library skills. Composition skills are necessary for written assignments such as research papers and essays.

Teachers tend to assume that students have the appropriate learning strategies for the social studies classroom. Social studies research, however, focuses on promoting strategic teaching and learning.

Teacher Considerations

Teachers must focus on the concepts that their students need to learn, not on the specific facts found in textbooks. Students need help to put the pieces of information into meaningful contexts. Teachers also need to include direct instruction of learning strategies needed for student success.

Social studies teachers should identify a student's inability to successfully read the textbook as a primary problem. Efforts need to be made to match students and prospective texts. And students need to learn how to use their social studies textbooks effectively.

Prereading activities, important to building appropriate background experiences for students, range from anticipation guides to audiovisual presentations and help students develop the background to successfully handle social studies reading. Varying student experience can be linked by providing a variety of materials on a topic or by using a number of different examples.

Assignments should be specific, and teachers need to provide clear direction as to *why* the material is being read, *how* it will be used, and *what strategies* would be most effective.

Model Lesson: Child Labor in America

Concept

This lesson focuses on a textbook reading concerning the growth of child labor laws and is designed for a ninth-grade U.S. history class. The textbook passage follows a problem/solution frame of organization. The students have been studying reforms advocated during the progressive era.

Preparation for Learning

PReP is a prereading strategy that helps the teacher identify what the students already know about a topic and provides a means to elaborate on these associations. The steps involve making initial associations with the concept, reflecting on these associations, and reformulating prior knowledge. The procedure also initiates an awareness that today's concept of childhood may not have been accepted in other historical contexts.

Procedure

1. *Initial Associations.* The teacher starts the lesson by asking, "Tell me what comes to mind when you think of the term, 'child labor.'" The teacher writes responses on the board. Examples could include sweat shop, work permit, hard work, minimum wage, miners, farming, and so on.
2. *Reformulation.* The teacher asks the individuals who contributed the responses, "What made you think of this?"
3. *Conceptualization.* The teacher then asks, "Based on our discussion, have you any new ideas about child labor?" The class discusses additional associations and comments (Langer, 1984).

Presenting the Content

The problem/solution grid is a strategy that ensures that students will actively read with a purpose. The problem/solution grid helps students identify the important elements of the content and gives them practice learning from the text by using this common organizational pattern.

The process of filling in the grid helps student to retain what they read. Students unfamiliar with this activity may need the teacher's help to identify the key problem in the text. Students with a great deal of experience can create their own grids that reflect the text structure (Alvermann, 1987).

Procedure

1. The teacher previews the reading, its content and its structure with students as a "think aloud." The teacher calls attention to the two pictures in the text, one of children in a textile factory and one of a child in a mine, and the headings that emphasize the various problems. The teacher explains how the passage follows a problem/solution format.
2. The teacher distributes the problem/solution grid and reviews its components. Students complete the grid as they read (Example 1).

Example 1

Problem/Solution Grid for "Child Labor in America"

Problem:	*Child labor in America was harmful to young people.*
Example 1	*Poor children did not experience "childhood."*
Example 2	*Children were frequently injured—mines and machinery.*
Example 3	*Fatigue—children were exhausted after work.*
Example 4	*Children suffered disease—tuberculosis.*
Example 5	*Illiteracy—children didn't go to school.*

Causes of the problem:

Cause 1	*There was a shortage in the labor force.*
Cause 2	*Industrial growth boomed after the Civil War.*
Cause 3	*Increase in number of immigrants—needed children to work.*

Actions taken by:

Group	*Progressives—Muckrakers and Reformers*

Solutions:

1. *Laws passed regulating working conditions, minimum age and hours.*
2. *1904 National Child Labor Committee formed.*
3. *1912 U.S. Children's Bureau established.*
4. *Journalists increased awareness of problem.*

Integration and Application

RAFT is a postreading activity that expands on the ideas encountered in the textbook reading. The writing, structured so students know their viewpoint, their audience, their format, and their purpose, encourages students to personalize a response to the ideas in the text and to flesh out the problems of child labor by drawing on their background knowledge. It also sets the stage for a discussion about appropriate legislative action (Santa, 1988).

Procedure

1. The teacher defines the RAFT assignment explaining the following elements:

   Role—you are the older sibling of a youth killed in a factory accident
   Audience—U.S. House of Representatives in 1912
   Format—testimony regarding a proposed federal child labor bill
   Topic—various problems connected with children in the work force

2. Students using their problem/solution grids should write a testimony that focuses on at least two problems connected with child labor. The statement should be at least two paragraphs.
3. The teacher calls on several students to read their testimony to the class.

The Learner in Vocational Subjects: Agriculture Education, Business Education, Family and Consumer Education, and Technology Education

Vocational subjects are, by definition, practical disciplines designed to prepare students for careers, consumerism, and daily living. Students in these subjects are often highly motivated to learn skills for their varied interests. In addition to job skills, the vocational subjects stress thinking skills, good work habits and attitudes, and the importance of adapting to new ideas and technologies in the work place. Learning tends to be experiential, with textbooks and supplementary materials providing a framework for learning.

Learner Considerations

The student in vocational subjects must learn the background, technical vocabulary, and necessary procedures for the discipline. However, students are often unprepared for learning that is process- and product-oriented and for technical reading that uses unfamiliar expository patterns. While students have been accustomed to focusing on main ideas and broad concepts, they also must learn a process' steps and pay attention to critical details. Students may have difficulty with common words that have different meanings in the technical vocabulary.

Students in agriculture education programs vary tremendously in educational abilities, vocational interests, and backgrounds. This variety requires teachers to give a great amount of attention to the differences. Instructors need to consider the reading abilities of their students and integrate a number of different strategies to assist comprehension of the text and supplemental reading. (See *A Guide to Curriculum Planning in Agriculture Education,* Wisconsin Department of Public Instruction, 1988.)

Business education programs offer instruction in all areas concerned with the sending and receiving of information as well as the reinforcement of communication skills. The business world demands that students make decisions rapidly and accurately and think logically and analytically. Students also must develop interpersonal skills necessary to handle change and complex lifestyles. (See *A Guide to Curriculum Planning in Business Education,* 1987; and *A Guide to Curriculum Planning in Marketing Education,* 1987; both published by the Wisconsin Department of Public Instruction.)

Family and consumer education provides students with skills for career development, employment, work in the family, and basic communication. The subject also emphasizes helping students develop reasoning skills, such as the ability to identify problems, propose and evaluate solutions, use inductive and deductive reasoning, and distinguish between fact and opinion. (See *A Guide to Curriculum Planning in Home Economics*, Wisconsin Department of Public Instruction, 1987.)

Learners in technology education must become technologically literate. They learn a variety of systems, the technical vocabulary for those systems, and the skills needed to perform certain operations or procedures. Learning in technology education is designed to be hands-on, activity-oriented, and learner-initiated. (See *A Guide to Curriculum Planning in Technology Education*, Wisconsin Department of Public Instruction, 1988.)

Text Characteristics

Textbooks in vocational subjects tend to be technical, focusing on rationales, directions, and descriptions. The teacher must provide demonstrations or explanations to give students the background knowledge they need to comprehend.

Textbook illustrations and visuals require interpretation that students are often unprepared to make. Thus, vocational teachers must assist their students in interpreting these visuals.

Teachers often bring in supplementary materials, such as brochures, pamphlets, articles, and magazines. These texts, usually written on highly technical levels, require background knowledge that students may not possess. For instance, agriculture and its related sciences are changing rapidly. To keep up with these changes teachers often update their materials. Frequently, these materials are highly technical and require appropriate support strategies in order for students to understand them.

Resources available for teaching business education reflect contemporary and innovative approaches about business. The materials include printed and computerized instructional techniques aimed at critical thinking and problem solving.

Material in family and consumer education offers a basis for comparative study and reflective thought. Teachers provide multiple resources that represent a variety of viewpoints. Besides student mastery of subject matter and factual information, students also must become critical readers and thinkers. Teachers should provide students with appropriate learning activities to help them make informed judgments, decisions, and actions involving family and work.

Resources for teaching technology education reflect the industrial approach to the four systems of technology—communications, construction, transportation, and manufacturing. Teachers should encourage students to use a variety of textbooks and journals when studying a concept in technology education. Technology education textbooks tend to be stimulating and include contemporary issues related to the field.

Context

Vocational subjects, characterized by activity-based instruction, require students to learn by doing. However, students sometimes become frustrated by having to read or listen to a description of a procedure or skill. Students might assume they know the material and jump to conclusions that could endanger their own or others' safety.

A wide range of reading, learning abilities, and motivation characterizes the typical vocational classroom. Students with good skills or high motivation may suffer if the teacher does not provide some individualized instruction. Teachers should encourage students to work cooperatively so that they can learn from each other.

Students in vocational subject classes operate at various skill levels, and vocational instructors must assist students with special learning needs. Teachers also might consider using cooperative learning, student tutors, individualized instruction, special projects, and other means to keep students interested and challenged.

Many technology education programs incorporate a station approach to teaching. Students rotate through various activities that offer the opportunity to explore a wide range of areas in a particular system. The stations, equipped with teacher-developed learning packets and equipment such as lasers, computers, robots, and electronic trainers, allow students of different abilities to succeed.

Evaluation of the process rather than the product is appropriate in family and consumer education. Informal assessment of critical reading and thinking can be done by noting the quality of class discussion, evaluating oral or written responses to critical reading assignments, and judging answers to critical reading and thinking problems.

Teacher Considerations

Teachers of vocational subjects need to determine which concepts need to be taught and the most effective ways to teach those concepts. They should identify the background knowledge of their students to help them see how new concepts relate to what they already know.

The teachers need to provide explicit instruction for learning strategies that will help students learn technical and special vocabulary, understand written text, and develop reasoning skills. In addition, students in vocational subjects often must act immediately upon their reading as they use equipment to prepare products and develop projects. Consequently, teachers must show students strategies for using reading as a tool to accomplish a task rather than learn information.

Teachers in vocational subjects may want to use cooperative learning and student tutoring to address varied levels of ability. These approaches are particularly valuable in vocational subjects because of the practical nature of the courses.

Teaching/Learning Strategies 9

Introduction

This chapter presents several teaching/learning strategies to help students become effective and independent learners. The chapter includes strategies appropriate for the three phases of strategic teaching: Preparation for Learning, Presentation of Content, and Integration and Application (see Chapter 6). The strategies in this chapter are organized according to the cognitive processes emphasized in each phase: activating/focusing strategies, selecting/organizing strategies, and integrating/applying strategies.

Several of the teaching/learning strategies presented in this chapter may be used during all three phases of strategic teaching. These strategies are categorized here in terms of the cognitive processes that represent the most important element of each strategy. For example, KWL Plus, which includes all six cognitive processes: activating, focusing, selecting, organizing, integrating, and applying, is listed under activating/focusing strategies because those processes are especially emphasized.

Teachers play a critical role in helping students become strategic learners through the use of teaching/learning strategies. Teachers need to continually emphasize the cognitive processes involved with each strategy as they work with students. If teachers present the steps and components of a strategy without helping students to truly understand why or how it works, they may not be able to help students alter a strategy when it doesn't work. Awareness goes beyond merely knowing the steps of a strategy to internalizing why the strategy works in specific situations. Thus, teachers need to teach these strategies in meaningful ways so that their students will apply the strategies independently and appropriately. (See Figure 5.)

Figure 5

The Strategic Learner

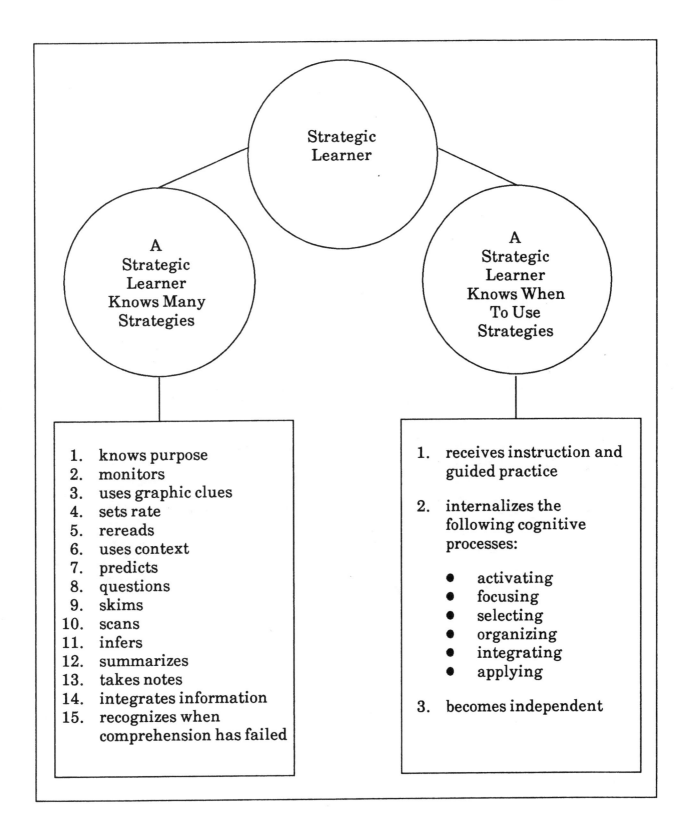

Strategic Learner

A Strategic Learner Knows Many Strategies

1. knows purpose
2. monitors
3. uses graphic clues
4. sets rate
5. rereads
6. uses context
7. predicts
8. questions
9. skims
10. scans
11. infers
12. summarizes
13. takes notes
14. integrates information
15. recognizes when comprehension has failed

A Strategic Learner Knows When To Use Strategies

1. receives instruction and guided practice

2. internalizes the following cognitive processes:

   - activating
   - focusing
   - selecting
   - organizing
   - integrating
   - applying

3. becomes independent

Figure 6

Teaching/Learning Strategies

Activating/ Focusing	Selecting/ Organizing	Integrating/ Applying
KWL Plus	Graphic Outlining	Reciprocal Teaching
LINK	Central Idea Graphic Organizers	Reading from Different Perspectives
PReP	Mapping	RAFT
Anticipation Guides	Proposition/Support Outlines	Framed Paragraphs
DRTA	Structured Notetaking	Four-Step Summary
Analogy Graphic Organizer	Semantic Feature Analysis	
Frayer Model	Vocabulary Overview Guide	
Word Maps and Charts	Think-Aloud	
	SMART	
	Interactive Reading Guide	
	Re Quest	

KWL Plus

Description

KWL Plus, a reading-thinking strategy, focuses on the student as a learner who asks questions and thinks about ideas while reading. The title derives from the three principal components of KWL—recalling what is known; determining what students want to learn, and identifying what is learned—plus mapping text and summarizing information.

Mapping and summarization were added to the original KWL strategy because writing and restructuring of text are powerful tools in helping students process information. The expanded strategy engages readers in constructing meaning from text and fosters student independence by developing their transfer skills. Students develop the ability to transfer, and thus to become independent learners, through instruction that gradually shifts the responsibility for initiating the strategy from the teacher to the student. After learning KWL Plus under teacher direction, students implement it on their own while receiving corrective feedback until they can complete the task independently.

Procedure

Step 1: Distribute copies of the KWL worksheet (sample included) to the class. Activate background knowledge. Guide students in brainstorming ideas and discussing what they know about the topic. As unanswered questions about specific points emerge, students can save them and refer to them later as information they want resolved when they read.

Step 2: After brainstorming and discussing, ask students to note on the KWL worksheets their knowledge of the topic. This forms the K (what is known) of the KWL technique.

Step 3: Guide students in categorizing their information. Help them to anticipate categories of information they may find in the article. By inducing a sense of expectation at the outset, KWL enhances student awareness of content and how it may be structured. Additionally, the categories enable them to anticipate and to relate information from other texts. Model the categorization process by thinking aloud while identifying categories and combining and classifying information. Students may then complete the "Categories of Information We Expect to Use" section on the worksheet.

Step 4: Guide students in generating questions as they read. Those questions become the basis for the W (what students want to learn). Questions can be developed from information gleaned in the preceding discussion and from thinking of the major categories of anticipated information. By developing questions in this manner, students learn to define independently their purpose for reading, which allows them to focus on the text and to monitor their learning.

Step 5: The text should be divided into manageable segments, at first by the teacher, then by the students as they become familiar with the technique. Depending upon an individual student's needs and abilities, one or two paragraphs may be all that a student can handle before he or she interrupts his or her reading and pauses to monitor comprehension by referring to the questions listed in column W. In this way, before the students read the entire passage, they become aware of what they have learned as well as what they have not comprehended.

Step 6: As students read and encounter new information, they can add questions to the W column. Thus, as students proceed through the material, they constantly think about what they read, monitor their learning, and perhaps generate additional questions to guide their reading. As they read, they also should note new information in the L (what students learn) column of the worksheet. This helps students select important information from each paragraph, and it provides a basis for future reference and review.

Step 7: Help students categorize the information listed under column L. Have students ask themselves what each statement describes. In doing so, they often discover more categories that can be used in future reading.

Step 8: Guide students in creating a map of the information. Through listing and categorizing, the most difficult tasks of constructing a map—i.e., selecting and relating important information from text—are already completed. Instruct students to use the article title as the center of their map. Categories developed with the KWL Plus worksheet become the map's major concepts, with explanatory details subsumed under each. Lines show the relationship of the main topic to the categories. All information categorized on the worksheet acts as supporting data on the map.

Step 9: Guide students in writing a summary of the material. The most difficult part of summarizing— selecting information and organizing it—has already been completed. Instruct students to use the map as an outline for their summary. Because the map depicts the organization of the information, a summary is comparatively easy to construct. The map's center becomes the title of the summary. Then students should number the categories on the map in the sequence they prefer. Each category forms the topic for a new paragraph. Finally, supporting details in each category are used to expand the paragraph or explain the main idea.

Sample KWL Worksheet

Topic _____		
K (Known)	**W** (Want to know)	**L** (Learned)

Final category designations for column L:

Categories of Information We Expect to Use

1.

2.

3.

4.

5.

6.

7.

Example 1: KWL Worksheet on Killer Whales

Killer Whales		
K (Known)	**W** (Want to know)	**L** (Learned)
They live in oceans. They are vicious. They eat each other. They are mammals.	Why do they attack people? How fast can they swim? What kind of fish do they eat? What is their description? How long do they live? How do they breathe?	D– They are the biggest member of the dolphin family. D– They weigh 10,000 pounds and get 30 feet long. F– They eat squids, seals, and other dolphins. A– They have good vision underwater. F– They are carnivorous (meat-eaters). A– They are the second smartest animal on earth. D– They breathe through blow holes. A– They do not attack unless they are hungry. D– Warm-blooded A– They have echo-location (sonar). L– They are found in the oceans.
Final category designations for column L, information learned about killer whales: A = abilities, D = description, F = food, L = location		

Categories of Information We Expect to Use

1. abilities

2. description

3. food

4. location

5.

6.

7.

Example 2: Concept Map on Killer Whales

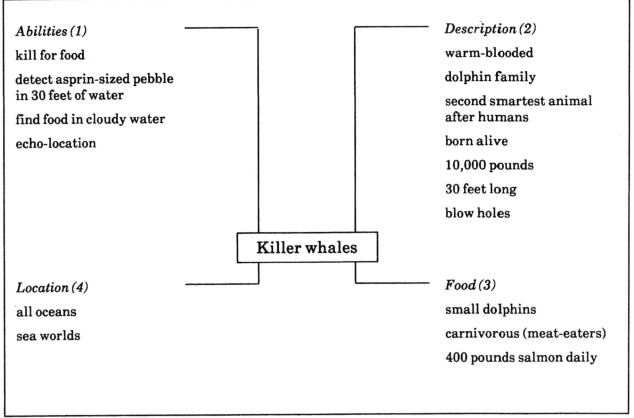

Abilities (1)

kill for food

detect asprin-sized pebble
in 30 feet of water

find food in cloudy water

echo-location

Description (2)

warm-blooded

dolphin family

second smartest animal
after humans

born alive

10,000 pounds

30 feet long

blow holes

Killer whales

Location (4)

all oceans

sea worlds

Food (3)

small dolphins

carnivorous (meat-eaters)

400 pounds salmon daily

(1) through (4) indicate the order of categories the student chose for writing a summary.

Student Summary

Killer whales are warm-blooded mammals and are part of the dolphin family. They are the second smartest animal after humans. Killer whales are born alive. They are 30 feet long and weigh 10,000 pounds. They breathe through their blow holes.

They are able to kill for food. They can detect a pebble the size of an aspirin tablet in a 30-foot tank. Killer whales also can feed in very cloudy water using echo-location. They eat as much as 400 pounds of salmon a day.

They are located in all oceans.

Reference

Carr, Eileen, and Donna Ogle. "KWL Plus: A Strategy." *Journal of Reading* (April 1987), pp. 626-631.

LINK

Description

LINK (List, Inquire, Note, Know), a preparation for learning strategy, is designed to help students link their prior knowledge with the information they will be studying. The inquiry phase of LINK prompts students to anticipate content and make associations. This activity cues students to their own prior knowledge and motivates them to study new material carefully.

Procedure

Step 1: Select a key concept or term that represents an important aspect of the material on which you intend to focus. Be sure it is a word that will trigger a response among the students.

Step 2: Display the key word on an overhead or a chalkboard.

Step 3: Ask the students to list their associations on paper. Allow three minutes for them to list their responses.

Step 4: Display their responses on the overhead or board. To maximize participation, ask for one response from each student in the class. You may want to call on less active participants first to increase chances of their involvement. Allow students to offer a second idea after everyone has responded.

Step 5: Have the students ask other students about items on the list. The teacher's role at this stage is largely passive and neutral. The purpose of this activity is to allow students to share and elaborate on their understandings. Let *them* discover their errors and difficulties.

Step 6: Turn off the overhead or erase the board. Then, instruct the students to turn over their papers and write down everything that comes to mind based upon prior experience and class discussion in response to the key word. Limit their brainstorming to one minute.

Reference

Estes, T., and J. Vaughn. *Reading and Reasoning Beyond the Primary Grades*. Boston, MA: Allyn and Bacon, 1986.

PReP

Description

PReP (Pre Reading Plan), a preparation for learning activity is designed to determine the extent of students' prior knowledge and experiences before they begin reading. Readers need appropriate prior knowledge about a topic or concept to be able to make inferences about it. PReP is valuable in helping teachers create a match between what the students know and the content and vocabulary of the text.

Procedure

Step 1: Preview the text or lesson and choose two to three important concepts.
Step 2: Conduct a brainstorming activity with the students to include the following phases.

Phase One: Initial association with the concept. "Tell me anything that comes to your mind when you hear the word . . . ." Jot ideas on the board. At this point, the students are making their first association between what they know and the topic.

Phase Two: Reflections on initial associations. "What made you think of . . . ?"
This step helps students develop an awareness of their network of associations and stimulates them to think of others. This process is called the multiplier effect. At this point, students may revise, weigh, accept, or reject their first associations.

Phase Three: Reformulation of knowledge. "Do have any new ideas about . . . ?" These responses are usually more refined than in phase one.

Step 3: Evaluate student responses to determine the depth of their prior knowledge of the topic. Langer and Smith-Burke (1982) identify three levels of response.

Level 1: Much prior knowledge. Students give superordinate concepts and definitions, make analogies, and link the concept with another concept. This level suggests students are able to comprehend the text without assistance.

Level 2: Some prior knowledge. Students give examples or attributes or define characteristics. This level indicates that students can make inferences about the topic and can comprehend the text with some teacher guidance.

Level 3: Little prior knowledge. Students respond with words that sound like the stimulus word or provide firsthand but not quite relevant experiences. This level of response indicates that students will not be able to form inferences or read with comprehension until they receive direct instruction about the concept.

Example: Science

Before an eighth-grade science class reads about photosynthesis in their texts, the teacher conducts a PReP activity to help the students recall and organize their knowledge of this concept and to determine which students are ready to read the material. The following dialogue focuses on the concept of photosynthesis. Other key words selected are "cycle" and "oxygen".

Phase 1: Initial Association of the Concept

Teacher: We're going to be reading in our texts about a process called photosynthesis. I'd like you to tell me anything that comes to mind when you hear the word photosynthesis. I'll write what you say on the board. Anyone?

During this phase, it becomes apparent that none of the students have much knowledge of the concept. The following is typical of the responses.

Responses	Response Level
Student 1: Sun shining on a plant.	Some: defining characteristic
Student 2: Photograph.	Little: morphemic association
Student 3: Pictures.	Little: morphemic association
Student 4: Something to do with science.	Little: association

Phase 2: Reflections on Initial Associations

Teacher: Now I'd like each of you to think about what you said and to try to tell us what made you think of that response.
Student 2: Photosynthesis sounds like photograph. The first part of it, anyway.
Student 3: Yeah, I thought at first you said photograph and that made me think of pictures.
Student 1: I remembered reading in a book about photosynthesis. There was this picture that showed rays coming out of the sun and going down to a plant. I just remembered the picture when I heard that word.
Student 4: I just remembered hearing the word in another science class.

During this activity, the teacher helps the group see that they do know something about the concept. A discussion grows out of the meaning of the photo morpheme and how it would be related to the sun and plants. This helps all of the students refine their responses in the third phase and helps some of them raise the level of their responses.

Phase 3: Reformulation of Knowledge

Teacher: Now that we've been thinking about this for a while, do any of you want to change or add to your previous responses, before we read about photosynthesis?

Student 1: It is when the sun shines on plants   Much: definition
and that helps the plants give oxygen.
Student 4: Sun and plants.   Some: defining characteristics

Students 2 and 3 still have only little prior knowledge, but they refine their previous responses by adding light, which they may have connected to their earlier photograph responses.

The teacher concludes that although Student 1 could successfully read the text, the others need help building the concept from what they knew before reading about it. Students 2 and 3 receive help to ensure that they understand the morpheme *photo* and the role of light in the process of photography. They then can extend this knowledge to the role of light in the process of the photosynthesis. Of course, further concept teaching takes place, but it always begins with the knowledge students display.

References

Langer, Judith. "Examining Background Knowledge and Text Comprehension." *Reading Research Quarterly* 19 (1984), pp. 468-481.

Langer, Judith and M.T. Smith-Burke, eds. *Reader Meets Author/Bridging the Gap: A Psycholinguistic and Sociolinguistic Perspective.* Newark, DE: International Reading Association, 1982.

Anticipation Guides

Description

Anticipation Guides are an effective way to activate thoughts and information about a topic. Before reading a selection, students respond to several statements that challenge or support their preconceived ideas relating to key concepts in the reading. Because student answers are based on their own thoughts and experiences, they should be able to explain and defend their positions in large- and small-group discussions. This process arouses student interest, sets purposes for reading, and encourages higher-level thinking—all important aspects of prereading motivation.

Students also are encouraged to make predictions about the major ideas in the selection before they start reading. Anticipation Guides also can be used after reading to evaluate how well students understood the material and whether or not misconceptions have been corrected. Anticipation Guides can be used in any content area and work equally well with print and nonprint media such as films and lectures.

Procedure

Step 1: Identify the major concepts and details in the reading. (What information or ideas should be the focus of the students' attention?)

Step 2: Consider student experiences or beliefs that the reading will challenge or support. (What do students already know or believe about the selection they will be reading?)

Step 3: Create three to five statements that may challenge or modify your students' prereading understanding of the material. Include some statements that will elicit agreement between the students and the information in the text.

Step 4: Present the guide on the board, on an overhead projector, or on paper. Leave space on the left for individual or small-group response. As each statement is discussed, students must justify their opinions. You may wish to have students first fill out the guide individually and then defend their responses to others in small groups or within a class discussion.

Step 5: After reading, return to the Anticipation Guide to determine whether students changed their minds regarding any of the statements. Have students locate sections in the reading that support their decisions.

Step 6: Another option for response is to include a column for prediction of the author's beliefs. This can be completed after students have read the selection and can lead into your discussion of the reading.

Example 1

Anticipation Guide: Memory

The following statements all concern memory and how your memory works. Place a check next to those statements with which you **agree**. Be prepared to defend your choices in a small-group activity by considering information you are familiar with and that supports your decisions.

_____1.   Some people undoubtedly have better memory abilities than others.

_____2.   Much of what we call intelligence is a good memory.

_____3.   The best way to put information into your memory is to keep going over it.

_____4.   If you understand what you read or hear, you will probably remember it.

_____5.   People can remember practically anything that ever happened to them when they are under hypnosis.

_____6.   People who appear to have super memory abilities are using some sort of memory trick.

Source: Doug Buehl, East High School, Madison (Wisconsin) Metropolitan School District, 1988.

Example 2

Anticipation Guide: Photosynthesis

_____Green plants cannot grow without sunlight.

_____Many plants get their food from the soil.

_____Photosynthesis only occurs in green plants.

_____Aquatic plants get their nutrients from water.

Source: Diane Hein, Cherokee Middle School, Madison (Wisconsin) Metropolitan School District, 1988.

Example 3

Anticipation Guide: Crash Was No Tragedy

Directions: Before you read Harris' article, check those incidents you think Harris will classify as tragedies in the column headed "You." Discuss your responses with class members, providing reasons for your choices. After reading the article, check in the column headed Harris those incidents that Harris would label as tragedy.

You   Harris

___   ___   1. In his desire to remain in office, a law-and-order president authorizes breaking the law (for political and national security reasons) and ultimately is driven from office.

___   ___   2. During the Master's Tournament, a golfer leading by ten strokes on the sixteenth hole of the last round is struck and killed by lighting.

___   ___   3. In Guatemala, an earthquake kills 16,000 people and leaves five times as many homeless.

___   ___   4. A mass murderer slips and falls to his death as police close in on him.

___   ___   5. A community spends $1 million to upgrade its football program instead of its airport, and then its football team dies in a crash at that airport.

___   ___   6. An understudy for an ill leading lady breaks her leg hurrying to meet her cue in her debut in a leading role.

___   ___   7. A father and mother of three die in a head-on auto accident on the way to work.

References

Moore, D.W., J.E. Readance, and R. Rickelman. *Prereading Activities for Content Area Reading and Learning.* 2nd ed. Newark, DE: International Reading Association, 1989.

Vacca, R.T., and J.L. Vacca. *Content Area Reading.* 2nd ed. Boston: Little, Brown, 1986.

DRTA

Description

The Directed Reading Thinking Activity (DRTA) is another excellent strategy to get students to make inferences while reading. The teacher's role is to guide students through a selection to help them formulate questions, make predictions, and validate or reject their predictions. The strategy should be taught over a period of time as the teacher gradually reduces guidance until the students begin to use the strategy independently.

Procedure

Step 1: Activate background knowledge. "Look at the picture and the title on the first page of the selection. Think about what you already know about this." Share ideas.

Step 2: Predict and set a purpose. "Predict what the selection will be about." "What do you think will happen next?" Support the prediction. "Why do you think so?" "What evidence do you find to support your prediction?"

Step 3: Read the selection silently. Remind students to keep their predictions and purposes in mind as they read.

Step 4: Confirm or reject the predictions. "What predictions can you prove?" "Why or why not?"

Step 5: Repeat the cycle with the next section of the selection.

Many teachers find it useful to write predictions and modifications on the board to focus the discussion as the students progress through the selection.

DRTA also can be considered a general instructional model for teaching as it integrates all the various strategies the reader uses before, during, and after reading. For example, the teacher might expand the third step to include using an opinion/proof strategy and follow up with application and integration activities that make use of this frame.

Example: Mathematics DRTA

Activate Background Knowledge

Ask students to examine the following figures in their textbook:

- scalene quadrilateral
- parallelogram
- rectangle
- square
- trapezoid and isosceles trapezoid
- kite

Predict and Set a Purpose

Guide students as they make predictions about the properties of each figure. For each figure, ask students to decide which of their listed properties led to the definition of the particular quadrilateral. Tell students to pay particular attention to the diagonals.

Read Silently

After completing the above tasks, have students read the appropriate section of the chapter.

Confirm or Reject Predictions

Guide students to compare their predictions of the properties of the figures with the definitions, theorems, and postulates in the text.

Have students draw each of the quadrilaterals discussed in the chapter and under each figure list the specific properties that make it a distinct geometric form. Students should include such properties as

- equal angles, sides, diagonals
- perpendicular parts
- supplementary
- bisections
- right angles

Extend Activities

Students solve the problem sets from the text for each subsection.

References

Santa, C.M. *Content Reading Including Study Systems*. Dubuque, IA: Kendall Hunt, 1988.

Wisconsin Department of Public Instruction. *A Guide to Curriculum Planning in Reading*. Madison, WI: Wisconsin Department of Public Instruction, 1986.

Analogy Graphic Organizer

Description

Analogies, an especially effective means to link familiar concepts with new information, are one option to many other strategies designed to help students examine the multiple meanings of words and concepts. This strategy also helps students broaden their understanding of key vocabulary or concepts as it introduces students to a new perspective or new relationship. Students must analyze simple to complex relationships between facts or concepts and use higher-level thinking skills as they comprehend the significance of the analogy.

Analogies are helpful when teachers

- activate background knowledge
- introduce new concepts
- explain ideas or describing relationships of facts
- show similarities between very different ideas
- strive to build student vocabulary knowledge

The basic structure of an analogy is the "relationship sentence" or question. Teachers should model the background or "hidden" thinking that is involved as a student strives to understand or write an analogy.

Students may not recognize how analogies can aid their understanding as they read or study. Teachers need specifically to point out any analogies in a text so that students will be aware of the function of analogies and their relationship to comprehension of content-area concepts.

There are many types of analogies. Some may highlight characteristics. For example,

"That car is a real dinosaur!"
"It's as hard as a rock."
"How is your nervous system like a telephone network?"
"How were the early French explorers like you on your first day of school?"

Some analogies highlight functions or help students relate new information to background knowledge (relating the "new to the known").

"Gills are related to fish as lungs are related to people."
"The propeller on a plane is like the flapping wings of an eagle."

Teachers can use analogies to introduce new topics and to evaluate student understanding of important concepts. Analogies also challenge student thinking. For instance, ask students to complete the following analogy:

"The cell is to the body as _____ are to a house." (Answer: bricks)

Procedure

Step 1. Determine what students know about possible analogous relationships involving the concept being introduced. Select one familiar concept to help the students develop an analogous relationship to the new concept.

Step 2. Use a compare/contrast graphic organizer with students to explore analogous as well as non-analogous characteristics of the two concepts. It may be necessary at this stage to brainstorm with students about specific characteristics or properties that may be common between the two concepts. Initially, this step is teacher directed using the graphic organizer on an overhead or chalkboard. As students develop more independence, individual copies of the graphic may be given to students for completion as a small group or individual exercise.

Sample Analogy Graphic Organizer

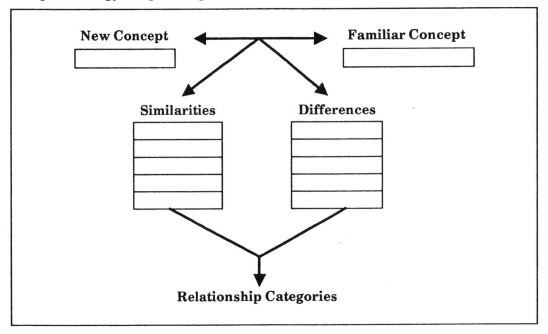

Step 3. Identify similarities and differences in the graphic organizer. Discuss with students the categories that make up the basis for the relationship. For example, when comparing volcanoes to popcorn, students will discover that their responses may be categorized as resulting from both heat and pressure. When comparing Ghandi with Martin Luther King Jr., students may observe that the categories representing the relationship categories are people's rights and methods of political activism.

Step 4. Relate the new concept to another familiar concept. Students should be guided in constructing their own analogies using these categories of relationships. This can be an effective way to encourage students to further explore and apply the key relationships to new situations. For example, when students discover that heat and pressure can cause an explosion, they could construct the following analogy: "Heat and pressure is to a volcano as a microwave oven is to a potato." Another example might be: "Ghandi was to Indian self-determination as Susan B. Anthony was to women's suffrage."

Example: Analogy Graphic Organizer for Social Studies

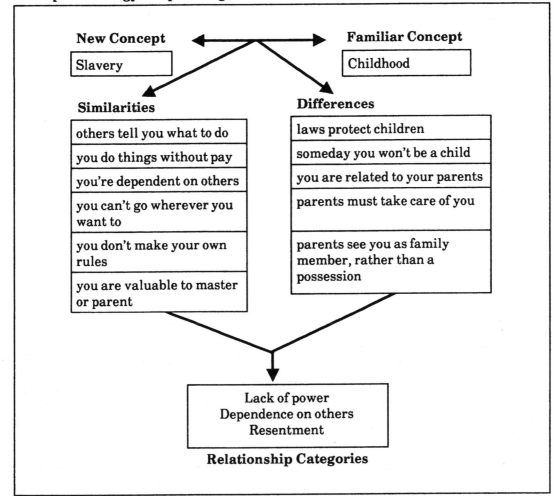

New Concept

Slavery

Familiar Concept

Childhood

Similarities

others tell you what to do
you do things without pay
you're dependent on others
you can't go wherever you want to
you don't make your own rules
you are valuable to master or parent

Differences

laws protect children
someday you won't be a child
you are related to your parents
parents must take care of you
parents see you as family member, rather than a possession

Lack of power Dependence on others Resentment

Relationship Categories

Reference

"Analogy Graphic Organizer." Based on unpublished work of Doug Buehl and Diane Hein, Madison (Wisconsin) Metropolitan School District, 1988.

Frayer Model

Description

The Frayer Model (Frayer, Frederick, and Klausmeier, 1969) is a graphic organizer that helps students learn precise meanings of key concepts. This model helps students select and organize information related to a key concept by focusing their attention on relevant details as they read. The Frayer Model's grid design facilitates differentiation of those characteristics necessary to the concept from those that are incidental or nonessential. Students then learn to identify examples as well as nonexamples of the concept.

Frayer Model

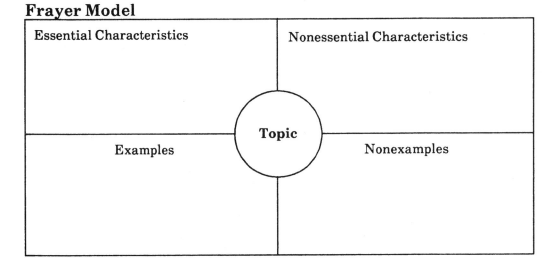

The Frayer Model has several advantages. The process helps students make connections between what they know and what they will be learning. Students learn how to examine a concept from a number of perspectives, how the concept relates to other concepts and information, and how to sort out the relevant features of a concept. The model also allows students to practice extending their knowledge of a concept by classifying more than one example of that concept. Students go beyond merely associating a key term with a definition, thus learning the content more thoroughly and improving retention of the information. The Frayer Model may be used before reading, during reading, or after reading to develop key concepts.

Procedure

Steps 1 and 2 of this procedure should be completed by the teacher before introducing the concept to the students. Steps 3 through 8 are modeled by the teacher with the entire class.

Step 1. Create a diagram that presents the concept in a hierarchical map. Include in this diagram supraordinate concepts (general classes of things), subordinate concepts (examples of a specific class), and coordinate concepts (parallel classes of things not directly a part of the concept). See Angiosperm Hierarchical example map on the following page.

Step 2. Define the concept carefully so that all relevant attributes are included. For example, if you were teaching the concept "mammal," your definition might be: "any vertebrate that feeds its young with milk from the female mammary glands, that has a body more or less covered with hair, and that, with the exception of the montremes, bears living young rather than eggs."

Step 3. Introduce the concept to the students by naming it and having students generate examples of the concept. One method would be to break the class into small groups and have students list as many examples of the concept as they can. After a short period, solicit the lists of examples and write them on the board or overhead transparency.

Step 4. Organize the examples into a map similar to the one developed in Step 1. Encourage students to add examples to the list or to challenge examples already offered. Many nonexamples will fit into this class map as coordinate (or parallel) concepts. For instance, if "eagle" and "chicken" are presented as examples of "mammal," these are added to the map under "bird," a parallel concept of "mammal." Students began to see the relationships between concepts.

Step 5. Finish the map by adding any of the important information identified on the map in Step 1. Explain why you place the terms where you do.

Step 6. Discuss with students the characteristics common to all the examples of the concept. These will be the relevant attributes you identified in Step 2. At this point, misconceptions can be corrected. For example, if all the student examples of the concept "elected officials in a democracy" are men, they might errantly conclude that "maleness" is a required characteristic.

Step 7. Guide the students in finding differences among the examples of the concept. These are the nonessential characteristics of the concept, those attributes that are not relevant to understanding the uniqueness of the concept. For example, "mammals" differ in their habitat, height, or weight; a "revolution" may be violent or nonviolent; a "poem" might rhyme, follow a meter, or be free verse; a "government" may be elected or unelected.

Step 8. Students are now ready to read material providing information about the concept. As the students read, encourage them to look for additional information that may be added to the their Frayer Model. Students should look for all information that will fit into any of the four categories (essential and nonessential characteristics, examples and nonexamples).

Step 9. As students develop familiarity using the Frayer Model, they can use it as a study guide to complete as they read.

Example: Hierarchical Map

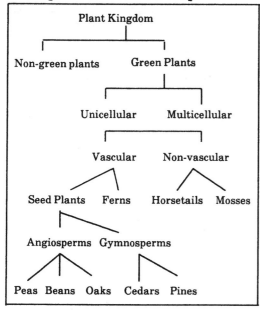

Example: Frayer Model for "Angiosperm"

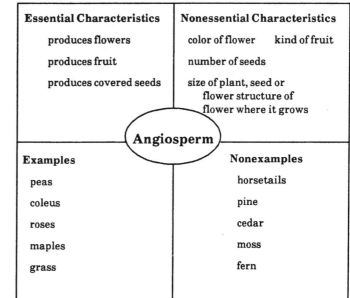

References

Frayer, Dorothy, W.G. Frederick, and Herbert Klausmeier. *A Schema for Testing the Level of Cognitive Mastery*. Working paper No. 16. Madison, WI: Wisconsin Research and Development Center, 1969.

Handbook on Reading in Content Areas. Orange County, FL: Orange County Schools, 1985.

Thelen, Judie. "Preparing Students for Content Reading Assignments." *Journal of Reading* (March 1982), pp. 544-49.

Word Maps and Charts

Description

Word maps and charts are graphic representations that help students visualize the components of a definition. The map includes three relationships essential to a rich definition:

- What is it?
- What is it like?
- What are some examples?

Word maps teach students the qualities of a definition. Too often, students have a narrow concept of what the meaning of a word encompasses. Many students think of definitions as simple, dictionary-like statements characterized by little elaboration and personal comment. Word maps encourage students to personally integrate their background knowledge with a concept. Once students understand the qualities of a definition, they apply this knowledge to expand their own vocabularies and to master unfamiliar concepts.

Procedure

Step 1: Explain to students that in order to understand new vocabulary, they need to know what makes up a definition of a word. Go over the three questions that make up a definition.

Step 2: Introduce students to the word map, and describe its parts. Begin with a familiar concept such as ice cream.

Step 3: Ask, "What is it?" (food, dessert). Write these descriptors on the map. (Tell students that their answers should be general.) Next, ask students, "What is it like?" Record their responses on the map (cold, creamy, delicious, soft, hard, etc.). Explain that these qualities are properties that make ice cream different from other foods and desserts.

Step 4: Ask for examples (chocolate, vanilla, strawberry, butter pecan, etc.). Encourage students to use information from their background experiences as they complete their maps.

Step 5: Model the process and guide the students through several other examples.

Step 6: Encourage students to use maps independently as they study. Tell them that word maps and charts help them to learn new, difficult concepts and that they can use them to study for exams.

Sample Word Map

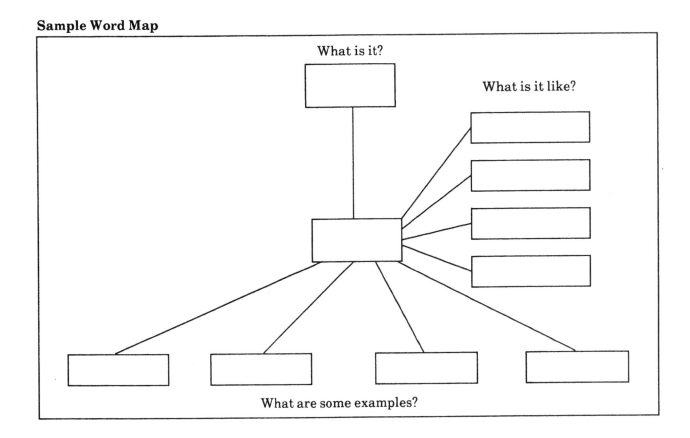

Example: "Ice Cream" Word Map

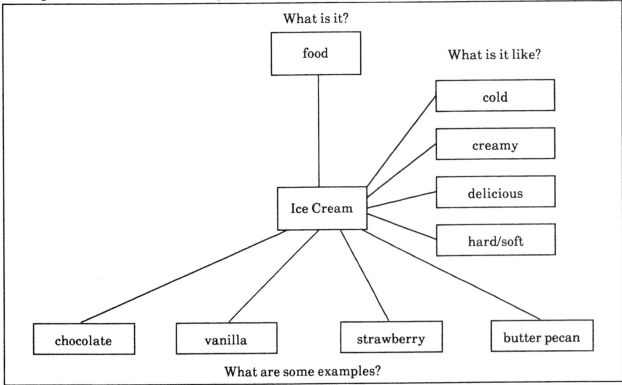

Reference

Schwartz, R., and T. Raphael. "Concept of Definition: A Key to Improving Students' Vocabulary." *The Reading Teacher* 39 (1985), pp. 190-205.

Graphic Outlining

Description

Graphic outlining helps students and teachers read and understand content-area texts. The outlining procedures consist of five basic steps: survey, represent, read with comprehension monitoring, outline, and summarize.

Graphic outlining is a way of representing the information in a text so that the structure of the text is highlighted. By creating graphic representations, the students predict what is likely to be important and organize the information they are learning. Graphic outlines are created to match the various organizational frames authors use in their writing (see Chapter 4). For example, by creating a compare/contrast graphic representation, the students determine which similarities and differences are likely to be important in a particular selection. As they read, the students select and organize information based on these similarities and differences. The graphic outline guides this comprehension process.

Procedure

Step 1: Survey

Model a survey of the selection. As part of this survey, students should

- examine the title, headings, graphics, and summary;
- look for clues as to the organization of the text; and
- ask questions, such as: How is the information structured? What do the questions seem to indicate as important information? Does the author compare or contrast two or more concepts? Is the text an explanation? Is there a cause-and-effect relationship indicated?

Step 2: Represent

Model the formation of hypotheses about the text's overall structure. Guide students as they determine the following:

- What frame questions seem most appropriate?
- What graphic structure would represent the structure most effectively?

During this step, the possible graphic outlines are simply predictions. If the students have a relatively clear picture of the overall structure, they may want to make simple drawings to use as a study aid. However, if the structure is unclear, it may not yet be possible to construct a graphic representation.

Step 3: Read with Comprehension Monitoring

Guide students as they read the selection using their tentative graphic outline. As part of this process, direct students to

- fill in gaps for understanding;
- look for ideas/areas not yet represented in the graphic;

- clarify any points raised during the reading by guiding students to reflect on their understanding of the reading; and
- check the graphic outline to see if it illustrates the important ideas and relationships of the reading.

Step 4: Outline
Model the completion of the graphic outline representations. Provide them with the sample graphic outlines as guides.

Step 5: Summary
Model the use of graphic outlines for writing summaries. Guide students through the process.

Example: Social Studies

The following example describes how a graphic outline might be applied to a third-grade social studies class. Their assignment is to read the chapter entitled "Cities as Communities."

Survey

The students look at the title, "Cities as Communities," and at the title page's pictures of New York City, Washington, D.C., and the interior of a garment factory. On succeeding pages are maps of the East Coast and of New York City. There also are pictures of children playing in a park and eight scenes in New York City. Students also look at the questions after each chapter subsection (e.g., "What are the five parts of New York City called?" "What is an apartment house?").

As students look for clues as to the organization of the text, they ask themselves questions such as how the information is structured, whether two or more concepts are being compared, and whether the text is an explanation.

Represent

The students form hypotheses about the text structure. In this case, the information seems to be simply an explanation of New York City. Thus, the first graphic representation is a spider map with New York City in the center. Its "location" and the "five parts" are subtopics. The students begin drawing a spider map.

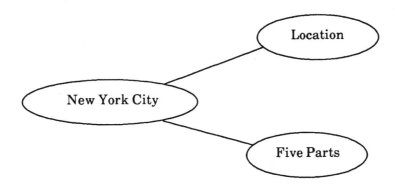

Read with Comprehension Monitoring

While the students read, they find the five boroughs of New York City, and they add them to the spider map. They also add subtopics related to downtown New York City and its neighborhoods.

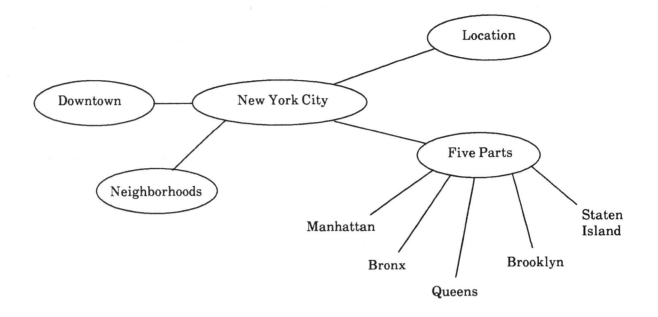

When they finish reading they reflect on whether the spider map shows the important structure of the chapter. They decide that it does, although they wonder if downtown and the neighborhoods are being compared.

Outline

Students complete the graphic outline. In this case, it is a spider map.

Summarize

The students write a summary to include the information from the chapter. They use the spider to help them write the summary.

Reference

Jones, B. F. "SPaRCS." In *Strategies for Teaching Reading as Thinking, A Teleconference Resource Guide*. Elmhurst, IL: North Central Regional Education Laboratory, 1988.

Central Idea Graphic Organizers

Description

Finding the central idea of a reading selection can be very difficult for many students. This strategy gives students a graphic format to organize their thoughts while looking for the main idea. It also lets students practice generating, rather than merely recognizing, a main idea from a reading selection. The graphic formats also serve to call attention to the text frames being used in the selection.

Generating the central idea can be either a during- or after-reading strategy. When using this strategy, it is important to teach students to differentiate between topics and main ideas. Explain that a topic is what the selection or paragraph is about and can be stated in one to three words. The main idea is what the author says about the topic and is stated in a sentence; it can be directly stated or inferred.

The reading task is more difficult when the main ideas are not explicitly stated in the material. Teachers should model this strategy first using material that has well-defined main ideas, then move on to paragraphs with inferred main ideas, and finally, show students paragraphs that don't have main ideas. Students should realize that text is not always written as explicitly as they may want it to be.

Procedure

Step 1: Ask the students to predict the topic of the entire selection from the title, its headings, illustrations, etc.

Step 2: After the students read the first paragraph, instruct them to decide on the topic and write it in the appropriate box in the graphic organizer.

Step 3: Ask the students to write on their graphic organizer what they learned about the topic. List the details in the appropriate boxes.

Step 4: Ask the students to state in a complete sentence, "What is the main thing the author says about the topic?" Instruct them to write it down in the appropriate box.

Step 5: The students should then check to see if all or most of the details connect with the main idea statement. If they don't, the student needs to get another main idea. If they do connect, move on to the next paragraph.

Reference

Caldwell, Jo Ann. From a course entitled "Strategies for Independent Reading." Cardinal Stritch College, Milwaukee, Wisconsin, March 1988.

Sample Central Idea Graphic Organizers

Descriptive Organizer

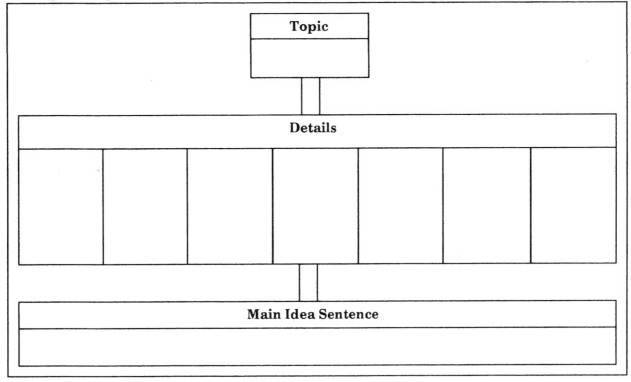

Problem/Solution Organizer

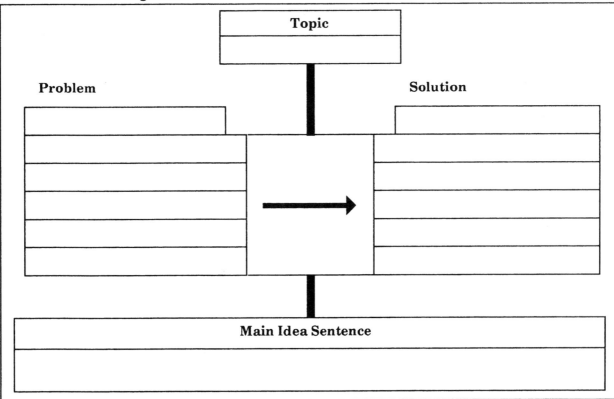

Sequential Organizer

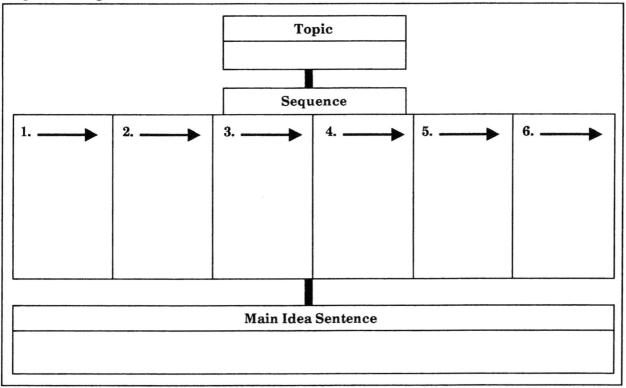

Compare/Contrast Organizer

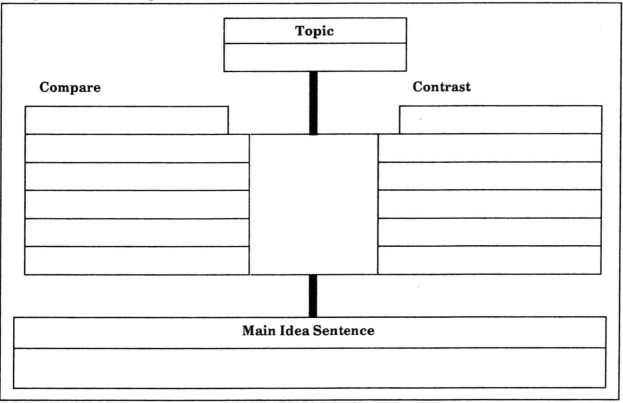

Example: Causation Graphic Organizer

Camels in the Desert

    Camels are still ridden by the people of the desert. They are well suited for carrying people and heavy burdens for long distances in hot, dry places because they can go for a long time without water. As a result of the thick hooves, camels can easily walk on the hot sand. Finally, camels can live in the desert because they are able to find even the smallest plant to eat hidden in the sandy soil.

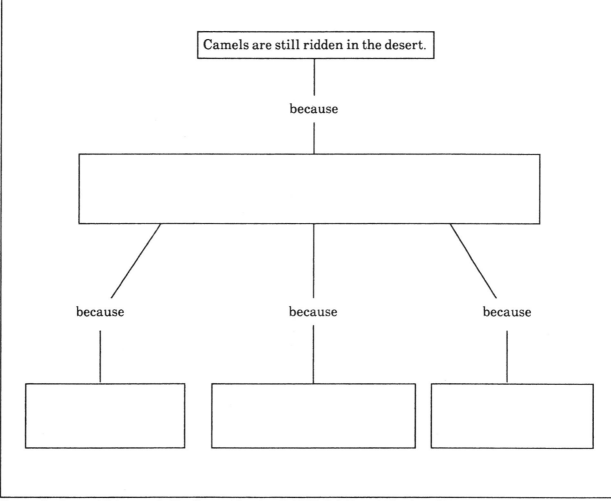

Source: *Professional Educators for Excellence in Reading (PEER)*, Vol. V, no. 1 (October 1988).

Mapping

Description

Mapping, a learning strategy that leads students to see connections between information or concepts, organizes words, ideas, or concepts in categories and shows how words relate to one another or how they go together. These maps (sometimes referred to as a mind maps or webs) help students link their prior knowledge to new ideas or vocabulary.

The center of the map contains the key word or concept, which is contained in either a geometric figure, such as a circle or square, or some sort of pictorial representation of the word or concept. Emanating from the central word or concept are the connecting links drawn in the form of lines or arrows. The related words or information are then written on these connecting lines. As the map grows outward from the center, the words or information become more specific and detailed.

While the mapping strategy can be used before, during, or after students read a selection, it is especially successful before reading to develop vocabulary. A vocabulary map builds students' backgrounds of important concepts by linking a key word or words with related words with which students are familiar. For example, before students read a rather difficult content selection containing a great deal of information and new vocabulary, a map could be constructed on the chalk board. This map also could serve as a graphic advance organizer, and as students read, the prior networking of new ideas would help them process the text more efficiently. The map helps students get the information "straight" and enables them to see how it fits together.

Maps help students organize concepts and focus on key words and supporting ideas. Through brainstorming with maps, the teacher can determine students' prior knowledge and can build on that knowledge. Creating a map also prompts students to become active participants in the classroom.

Procedure

Step 1: Select a key word or concept from the selection the students will be reading. Write it in the center on the board, on an overhead transparency, or on a piece of paper, and circle it.

Step 2: Brainstorm with the students about what they already know about this concept, and have them hypothesize what the basic categories of information will be in the reading passage.

Step 3: Guide students to survey the reading, and check the accuracy of their predictions. Write the categories on the map and connect them with lines to the concept in the center. Students should do the same with the individual maps they create.

Step 4: Guide students to read the text and complete their maps by adding information to each category. You may instruct students to read the text in parts, stopping after each section to place the relevant information on their maps. Students then review the section to check if they missed any important information and to add it to their maps.

Step 5: Be creative. Encourage students to use words, pictures, phrases, circles, rectangles, colors, or anything else that may help them portray the concepts as they create their maps.

Step 6: Discuss the ideas contained in the student maps. Have the students use their maps to review for a quiz or test, to write a summary of the material, or for some other activity that involves applying and extending the concepts from the text.

Example 1

"Bookworm" Map

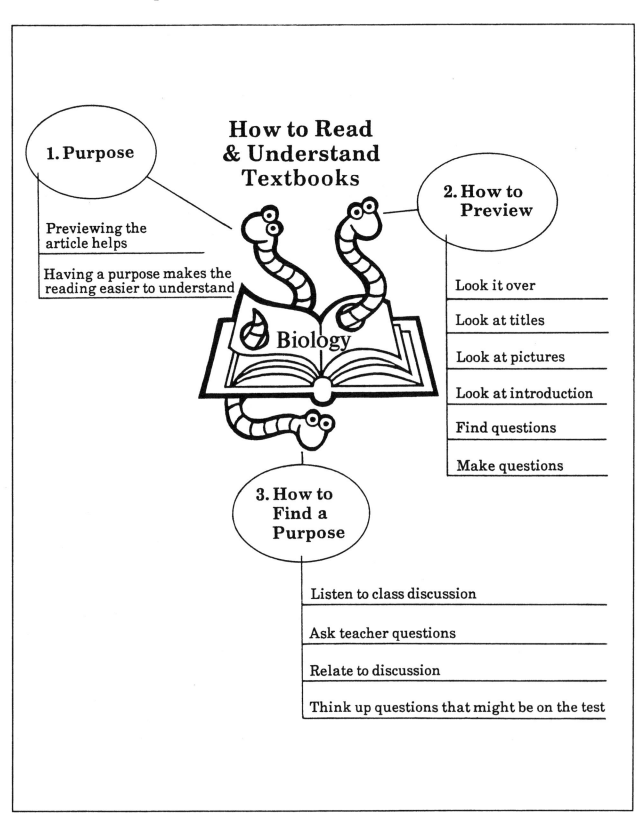

How to Read & Understand Textbooks

1. Purpose

Previewing the article helps

Having a purpose makes the reading easier to understand

Biology

2. How to Preview

Look it over

Look at titles

Look at pictures

Look at introduction

Find questions

Make questions

3. How to Find a Purpose

Listen to class discussion

Ask teacher questions

Relate to discussion

Think up questions that might be on the test

Example 2

"Classifying Triangles" Map

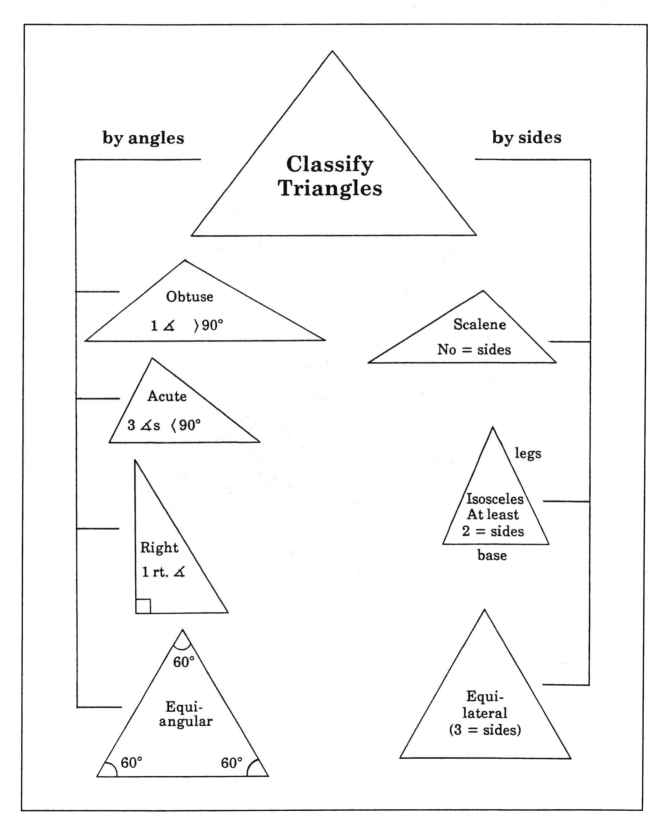

Example 3

Social Studies Map

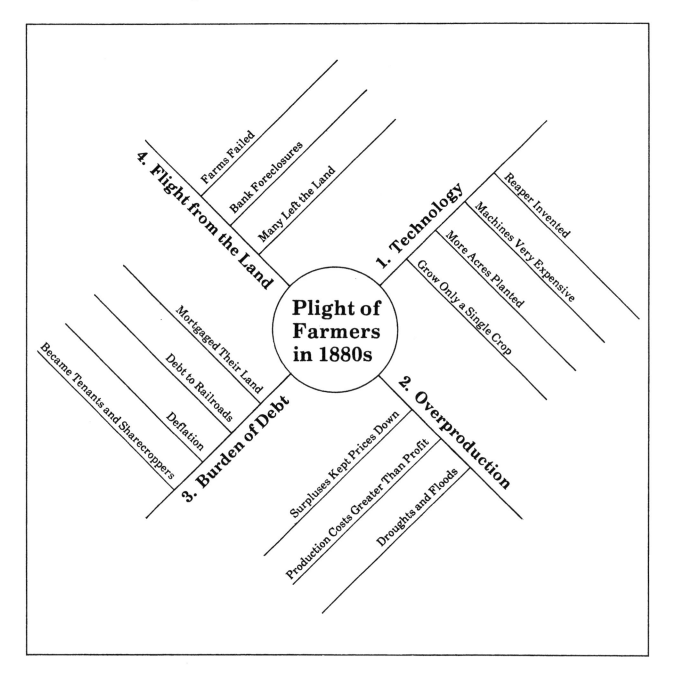

Reference

Heimlich, J. E., and S. D. Pittelman. *Semantic Mapping: Classroom Applications.* Newark, DE: International Reading Association, 1986.

Johnson, D.D., and P.D. Pearson. *Teaching Reading Vocabulary.* New York: Holt, Rinehart and Winston, 1984.

Wisconsin Department of Public Instruction. *A Guide to Curriculum Planning in Reading.* Madison, WI: Wisconsin Department of Public Instruction, 1986, pp. 104-105.

Proposition/Support Outlines

Description

Proposition/support (or opinion/proof) outlining is an organizational system that teaches students how to support an argument with evidence. Students find this format useful for organizing information from reading assignments and for prewriting activities.

Students can use proposition/support outlining before, during, or after reading. It provides them with a structure that helps them organize their thinking, writing, and classroom discussions. Students can develop their own opinion and find evidence for support, or the teacher can give the students a statement to prove. This strategy helps students develop and use higher level thinking skills and is appropriate in all content areas.

Procedure

Step 1: Direct the students to divide their paper into two columns and label the columns "proposition" and "support" or "opinion" and "proof." Do the same on an overhead transparency or the chalkboard.

Step 2: Have students read the assigned selection.

Step 3: Model the strategy for students by developing a proposition or opinion statement based on the selection.

Step 4: Show students how to support this statement with details from the selection. Add these details to the support column on the class outline on the overhead or chalkboard.

Step 5: Have the students develop their own propositions or opinions from the selection and find evidence in the selection to support it. Guide them on using the outlines as a framework.

Step 6: Guide the students as they construct a summary paragraph based on the proposition statement and the details that support it. Eventually students may use their outlines to write longer position papers.

Step 7: Guide the students in analyzing their summaries by using a checklist.

Sample Proposition/Support Checklist

_____ Is my statement clear?

_____ Do I need more evidence to support my statement?

_____ Is my most convincing fact placed in a position in my paragraph that will make it stand out clearly?

_____ Could I move my facts around in a way that would make my ideas clearer to my readers?

Example 1: Social Studies Proposition/Support

Proposition	Support
Constitutional convention was necessary	Articles of Confederation were weak and caused concern about the new government. Trade between states was problem; colonies competed with one another. Lack of power over foreign trade; no central government with power to impose tariff. Lack of power to enforce treaties; foreign countries did not recognize American government.
Conclusion	The Articles of Confederation had to be revised because of its weakness. The country needed a new executive branch, a judicial branch, and a strong central government.

Example 2: Social Studies Opinion/Proof

Opinion	Proof
Napoleon was a great leader.	1. ended revolution 2. drew up new constitution 3. fair taxation 4. government workers chosen for ability

Supporting Summary

Napoleon was a great leader. He brought an end to the revolutionary fighting in France and then established a national police force to keep peace. He told all the nobles who had fled the country during the fighting that they could return home. Napoleon also drew up a new constitution that gave all male citizens the right to vote. All citizens, including the rich, were made to pay taxes and government workers were chosen for their ability. It did not matter who they were. And last, but not least, he led the military to many victories.

Opposing Summary

Napoleon was not a great ruler. He cost France many lives during all those wars when he tried to rule the world. The people who had run away during the revolution could only come back to their homes if they supported him. Also, he only allowed men to vote; he didn't think women would do a good job.

Example 3: English Opinion/Proof

Opinion	Proof (including supporting details)
Kino in *The Pearl* was selfish and chauvinistic.	He sat outside while Juana, his wife, did all of the work.
	He made decisions for the family without consulting her.
	For example—He decided to keep pearl, decided to bury pearl, wanted rifle, ended up using it to destroy the thing he loved most.
	He did not accept advice from friends and family.
	He would not listen to brother and other villagers.

Example 4: Science Proposition/Support

Proposition	Support
There should be more habitat for grizzly bears.	Grizzlies are a threatened species. Problem caused by hunters, people encroaching on habitat.
	Logging operations decrease grizzly habitat in Forest Service lands.
	Hiking, camping, and hunting activities interfere with grizzlies.
Conclusion	Human activities that interfere with grizzlies should be limited.

Reference

Santa, C.M., *Content Reading Including Study Systems*. Dubuque, IA: Kendall Hunt, 1988.

Structured Notetaking

Description

Structured notes are graphic organizers that reflect the text structure the author used or the structure the reader inferred.

Readers who generate structured notes use common text structures as an organizing framework for their notes. They organize their notes around main ideas and the relationships of those main ideas to important details. This notetaking system contrasts with a simple listing of ideas in the order in which they appear in the reading.

Procedure

Step 1: Discuss with students notetaking techniques and problems that they may have in taking notes. Point out that many students have difficulty taking notes, such as trouble in deciding what to include or how to organize notes. Tell students that they will be learning a strategy that may help them take notes.

Step 2: Introduce one text structure strategy (begin with time/order) and show examples of that structure in simple, short passages of text from a content-area textbook. Select passages that clearly exemplify and signal the structure, and point out the cue words and phrases that signal the structure.

Step 3: Present the graphic organizer (see Chapter 4) for that structure. Guide students by

- telling them how the organizer represents the structure pictorially and
- entering main ideas and details from the passage onto the organizer to complete it.

Explain that they soon will be creating their own notes in this form, not just filling in already existing notes.

Step 4: Repeat the process with two more structures. Indicate differences between structures. Guide students to

- identify these three structures in simple, clearly signaled, short prose segments and
- draw graphic organizers, and enter main idea and detail phrases on them.

Provide feedback, encourage students to tell why they identified a segment as representing that structure and why they included particular information on the organizer.

Step 5: Repeat Step 4 with the remaining structures. Review all the structures and provide additional practice identifying the structure in passages in which the structure is merely implicit (e.g., without cues in introduction, headings, or transitions).

Step 6: Use an explicitly structured passage approximately five to ten paragraphs long from a content-area textbook. Model the notetaking strategy using a read/think-aloud procedure (Flower and Hayes, 1981). Explain the purpose for reading the passage and scan it. Comment whenever the overall structure becomes evident. Use the structure to predict subsequent content and rectify misconceptions that arise as you encounter new information. Continuously scan ahead and back to check on ideas that support the structure.

Create a structure-based graphic organizer, filling in main idea and detail information, fleshing out the graphic summary by referring back to text, and adding pictorial cues to represent main idea or important detail information. When filling in the organizer, paraphrase rather than using the text verbatim.

Step 7: Provide one explicitly structured and one implicitly structured three-to five-paragraph expository passage. Ask students to pair up and practice the notetaking strategy using the read/think-aloud procedure, starting with the explicitly cued passage. One student reads the passage aloud and takes notes, describing his/her mental processes orally. The partner provides feedback and encouragement. Then students switch roles and work with the implicitly cued passage.

Step 8: Introduce a full chapter of expository material that has explicitly cued, clear combinations of structures. It may be necessary to revise existing materials to have such a clean-cut example. Model the notetaking strategy using the read/think-aloud technique. Create a graphic organizer that encompasses the combinations of structures included in the chapter. Point out that there is no single correct form of organizer, but that the organizer that is developed should present the top-level structure as well as the other structures used in the passage.

Step 9: Provide students with a chapter of explicitly cued and cleanly structured expository material that they have not encountered previously. In pairs, have them generate a graphic organizer. Collect and review the structured notes that they produce and choose 2 or 3 to discuss and evaluate in a subsequent lesson. In the discussion, provide feedback on selection of structures, page layout, and selection of main ideas and details included on the organizer. Next, have students complete a similar activity independently.

Step 10: Model the read/think-aloud procedure using the notetaking strategy with implicitly structured and poorly organized materials. Show students alternative structures that might be used in creating graphic organizers and discuss how alternate structures emphasize different points. Have students practice the notetaking strategy with implicitly cued and poorly organized chapter-length materials.

Reference

Smith, Pat, and Gail Tompkins. "Structured Notetaking: A New Strategy for Content Area Readers." *Journal of Reading* (October 1988), pp. 46-53.

Sample Types of Graphic Organizers for Common Text Structures

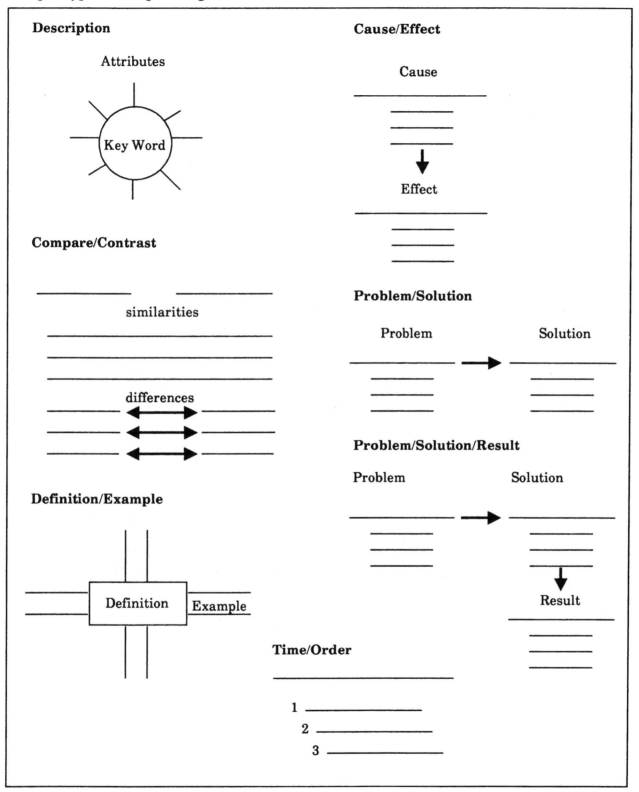

Description

Attributes

Key Word

Cause/Effect

Cause

Effect

Compare/Contrast

similarities

differences

Problem/Solution

Problem   Solution

Problem/Solution/Result

Problem   Solution

Definition/Example

Definition   Example

Result

Time/Order

1
2
3

Semantic Feature Analysis

Description

Semantic feature analysis uses charts and grids to help students explore how related words differ from one another. By analyzing semantic features of words, students can master important concepts that will help expand their vocabulary and help them understand words essential to learning concepts in content areas.

Procedure

Step 1: Identify the topic category to be analyzed.

Step 2: On an overhead transparency or on the chalkboard, list in a column some words related to the topic category.

Step 3: List in a row across the top of the chart some features shared by some of the words.

Step 4: Model with students an analysis of each related word in terms of each feature. Put plus or minus signs beside each word beneath each feature according to the appropriate relationship.

Step 5: Brainstorm with students for additional words that may be added to the column.

Step 6: Brainstorm with students for additional features that may be added to the row.

Step 7: Complete with students this expanded matrix with plus and minus signs.

Step 8: Discover and discuss with students the uniqueness of each word.

Example 1: Science

This example is from a fourth-grade science class.

1. A category is selected (types of rocks).
2. Some words within the category are listed in a column. In this example, the words include *granite, obsidian, limestone, coal, shale, slate,* and *gneiss.*
3. Some features shared by some of the words are listed in a row across the top of the chart. In this example, *formed by fire, changed by heat or pressure,* and *formed from other rocks* are listed.
4. Plus and minus signs are placed beside each word beneath each feature (see chart).
5. Additional words are added (e.g., *basalt, sandstone*).
6. Additional features are added (e.g., *with large crystals, black, containing fossils*).
7. The matrix is completed with plus and minus signs.
8. The words are discussed so that students see how the words are similar as well as how they differ. (e.g., Granite is a rock that has large crystals and is formed by fire).

Example 1: Semantic Feature Analysis for Types of Rocks

Rock	Formed by Fire	Changed by Heat and Pressure	Formed from Other Rocks				
granite	+	–	–				
obsidian	+	–	–				
limestone	–	–	+				
coal	–	–	+				
shale	–	–	+				
slate	–	+	–				
gneiss	–	+	–				

Example 2: Semantic Feature Analysis for Biology

Chordata	Reptile	Amphibian	4 Legs	Scaly	Clawed Feet	Cold Blooded	Lungs
turtles	+	–	+	+	+	+	+
lizards	+	–	+	+	+	+	+
snakes	+	–	–	+	–	+	+
alligators	+	–	+	+	+	+	+
crocodiles	+	–	+	+	+	+	+
frogs	–	+	+	–	–	?	?
toads	–	+	+	–	–	?	?
salamanders	–	+	+	–	–	?	?

Reference

Johnson, D.D., and P.D. Pearson. *Teaching Reading Vocabulary.* New York: Holt, Rinehart and Winston, 1984.

Vocabulary Overview Guide

Description

The Vocabulary Overview Guide provides a structure that students can use as they learn new, more difficult concepts. The strategy helps students develop an association with a significant clue to a word's meaning as well as determine its definition. The Vocabulary Overview Guide is especially valuable in that it encourages students to list descriptive statements in their own words and focuses their attention on the important categories related to the main topic of a selection.

The Vocabulary Overview Guide can be used successfully to build vocabulary in all content areas and is particularly appropriate when starting a new unit or studying for tests.

Procedure

Step 1: Model the use of the Vocabulary Overview Guide on an overhead transparency or chalkboard. Guide students to follow along as they fill in their own copy. This process can be used both before and after students read a text.

Step 2: Identify with students the main topic of the selection. The main topic may be signalled by a chapter title or if a segment of a chapter is being read, by a heading or subheading.

Step 3: Identify with students the important categories of information within this main topic through a preview of the selection to be read. For example, if the main topic is "rocks," categories may include "igneous," "metamorphic," and "sedimentary."

Step 4: Select the first category discussed in the reading and guide students as they skim to identify new and difficult words related to this category. Add these words to their vocabulary overview guide.

Step 5: Complete with students the definition for one of their words. Using information from the text, students should write the word's definition on the designated lines.

Step 6: Model the linking of this definition with the students' background knowledge. Guide students as they decide upon a personal clue that connects the word with something they already know.

Example Clues

Word: granite   Clue: *grey & Rocky Mts.*

Word: rambunctious   Clue: *my cousin Jerry*

Step 7: Guide students as they develop the definitions and clues for the rest of the words.

Step 8: Guide students as they use the Vocabulary Overview Guide to study. Students may be assigned to work with a partner as they use the guide to learn the new words. Model the studying of each word by first revealing only the word, then uncovering the clue if needed, and finally uncovering the definition.

Step 9: Encourage students to continue to add to their definitions as they learn more about each word. In this way, they will connect known words with new words, and that will help them to remember.

Sample Vocabulary Overview Guide

Main Topic _____

Category _____

Word: _____

Clue:

Definition(s): _____

_____

_____

_____

_____

Word: _____

Clue:

Definition(s): _____

_____

_____

_____

_____

Word: _____

Clue:

Definition(s): _____

_____

_____

_____

_____

Word: _____

Clue:

Definition(s): _____

_____

_____

_____

_____

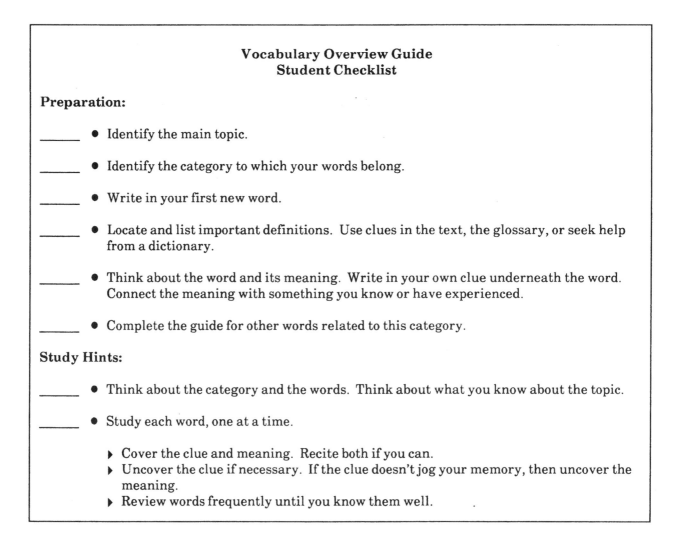

Vocabulary Overview Guide
Student Checklist

Preparation:

_____ • Identify the main topic.

_____ • Identify the category to which your words belong.

_____ • Write in your first new word.

_____ • Locate and list important definitions. Use clues in the text, the glossary, or seek help from a dictionary.

_____ • Think about the word and its meaning. Write in your own clue underneath the word. Connect the meaning with something you know or have experienced.

_____ • Complete the guide for other words related to this category.

Study Hints:

_____ • Think about the category and the words. Think about what you know about the topic.

_____ • Study each word, one at a time.

  ▸ Cover the clue and meaning. Recite both if you can.
  ▸ Uncover the clue if necessary. If the clue doesn't jog your memory, then uncover the meaning.
  ▸ Review words frequently until you know them well.

Example Vocabulary Overview Guide

Main Topic Progressive Movement

Category Reforms

Word: initiative

Clue: start

Definition(s):

introduce

legislation

Word: primary

Clue: early

Definition(s):

a "nominating election"

Word: suffrage

Clue: ERA

Definition(s):

Right to vote

Word: recall

Clue: take back

Definition(s):

a procedure for

removing from office

References

Caldwell, Jo Ann. From a course entitled "Strategies for Independent Reading." Cardinal Stritch College, Milwaukee, Wisconsin, March 1988.

Carr, E. "The Vocabulary Overview Guide." In *Strategies for Teaching Reading as Thinking*. Elmhurst, IL: Association for Supervision in Curriculum Development, 1986.

Think-Aloud

Description

Think-alouds model the kinds of strategies a good reader uses. Think-alouds teach students to generate queries that help them monitor and regulate their understanding as they read. The process encourages students to focus on getting meaning by anticipating, monitoring, and checking (thinking about your thinking). Think-alouds are an especially effective method to model specifically what a good reader does to cope with a particular comprehension problem.

The teacher who uses think-alouds models the following self-questioning strategies.

Prior to Reading

- What are my purposes for reading?
- What will I be doing with this information?
- What do I already know about this topic?
- What do I think I will learn about this topic?
- What are my predictions?

During Reading

- Am I understanding? Does this make sense? Do I have a clear picture in my head?
- Is this what I expected? What parts are different or similar to my predictions?
- What can I do to increase my understanding?

After Reading

- What were the most important points of the material? Which sections of text support them?
- How do I feel about this information? Do I disagree?
- What new information did I learn? How does it fit with what I already know?
- Should I go back and reread portions for better understanding? Should I use "fix-up" or memory strategies?

Procedure

Step 1: Select a passage to read aloud that contains points of difficulty, contradictions, ambiguities, and/or unknown words. Have students follow along silently as you read.

Step 2: Make predictions as you read aloud so that the students see how you develop hypotheses about the material. *"How am I supposed to solve this problem? What is the problem? I need to know how many more boxes Jane has to sell to reach her goal. What do I know—her goal is 42, and she has already sold 25 boxes—I think I will find her goal by either subtracting or adding."*

Step 3: Describe the picture you're forming in your head from the information. This step demonstrates how to develop images during reading. *"I have a pile of 25 boxes of Girl Scout cookies on one side. Most are mint with that waxy chocolate, some are peanut butter, and there are a few Scott Teas. Then, I have an empty space with a question mark. Then, I have an equal sign, and on the other side of the equal sign, I have a pile of 42 boxes of all kinds of Girl Scout cookies."*

Step 4: Share an analogy by showing students how to link prior knowledge with new information in the text—the "like-a" step. *"We did a problem like this yesterday when we . . . and we did . . . ."*

Step 5: Talk through a confusing point to model how you monitor your ongoing comprehension. *"Do I need to add or subtract here? Let's see, I need to know what number of boxes plus what number of boxes equals 42 boxes. So, I must add. No, that can't be right because 25 and 42 equals 67, and that is more than Jane's goal. I better reread. I must have to subtract the number of boxes Jane has already sold from the number of boxes that is her goal."*

Step 6: Demonstrate fix-up strategies that may be used to clear up confusion. Model rereading, reading ahead, looking for context clues for unknown words, and other similar strategies.

Step 7: Allow students to share their reactions to the text. After several modeling experiences, have students work with partners to practice think-alouds.

Step 8: Encourage students to practice thinking through materials on their own. Reinforce these thinking strategies with selected reading lessons and content reading.

References

Davey, B. "Helping Readers Think beyond Print through Self-Questioning." *Middle School Journal* (November 1985), pp. 38-41.

Davey, Beth. "Think Aloud—Modeling the Cognitive Processes of Reading Comprehension." *Journal of Reading* (October 1983), pp. 44-47.

SMART

Description

SMART, Self-Monitoring Approach to Reading and Thinking, can significantly improve student comprehension by reinforcing that learning begins with an identification of what one understands and what one does not understand from reading. This strategy encourages students to think rather than memorize by providing them with a monitoring process to apply during reading. Students find this strategy easy to apply, and after a few trials, they realize that they can substantially increase their understanding. However, when using SMART, students may ask for help too quickly without attempting a solution for themselves. Therefore, two things should be required of students as they ask for help. First, students should be able to specify the source of difficulty; second, they should be able to explain what they have done to try to unravel the puzzle.

Classroom environment and the context of the lesson are very important when students use this strategy. Because students are encouraged to admit they are not understanding, SMART involves a degree of risk-taking on their part. The teacher needs to communicate clearly that comprehension breakdowns are a normal part of reading and that successful learners recognize their breakdowns and remedy them.

Procedure

Step 1: Place a sample passage on an overhead.

Step 2: Model the SMART process through a think-aloud. Use the following steps:

- While reading,
  —place a check (√) in the margin while reading if you do understand.
  —place a question mark (?) in the margin if you do not understand.
- After each section, explain to yourself in your own words what you do understand (you may look back).
- Examine ideas that you did NOT understand.
  —Reread parts that you did not understand.
  —Specify the cause of the problem.
  —Think of something you might do to help yourself understand.
  —Try to explain ideas that you do not understand.
- Study using these steps. After reading the entire assignment,
  —close the book and explain what you do understand,
  —look back and refresh your memory,
  —reexamine those ideas you do not understand, then
  —close the book one last time and explain what you do understand.

Reference

Estes, T., and J. Vaughan. *Reading and Reasoning Beyond the Primary Grades.* Boston, MA: Allyn and Bacon, 1986.

Interactive Reading Guide

Description

The Interactive Reading Guide requires students to work cooperatively as they read and learn from text. The teacher directs the strategy much like a conductor leads an orchestra—sometimes requiring responses from individuals, pairs, small groups, or the entire group. The interactive reading map encourages the process. Instead of merely answering literal questions or filling in blanks, students are asked to predict, develop associations, read to a partner, reorganize information according to the text's structure, or summarize the reading. After individuals or groups complete each segment or part, the class as a whole discusses their responses. As can be seen in the following example, the culminating activity involves a mental and then written review of the selection's major concepts, events, or characters. Learning guides should be used for portions of text that may be difficult or that are designed specifically to capitalize on the advantages of cooperative learning. The guides should include opportunities for student-to-student and student-to-teacher interactions.

Procedure

Step 1: Direct the students to skim the interactive guide and the text before setting a purpose.

Step 2: Explain and model the skills and strategies before the students work independently. Go through the guide with the students so they can understand how such guides can help them learn.

Step 3: Circulate among students and monitor their work. This allows teachers to coach individuals or groups and to determine which students may need further encouragement.

Step 4: Follow up with a discussion instead of merely asking for assignments. These discussions of guide responses can increase interest, learning, and recall.

Step 5: Avoid assigning grades. The finished guide is often the result of group effort and developed to assist students with the reading.

Step 6: Encourage strategic reading. Strategic readers read with purpose and direction, and they know what strategies to use and when to use them.

Reference

Wood, Karen. "Guiding Students through Informational Text." *The Reading Teacher* (May 1988), pp. 912-918.

Example Interactive Reading Guide: Social Studies

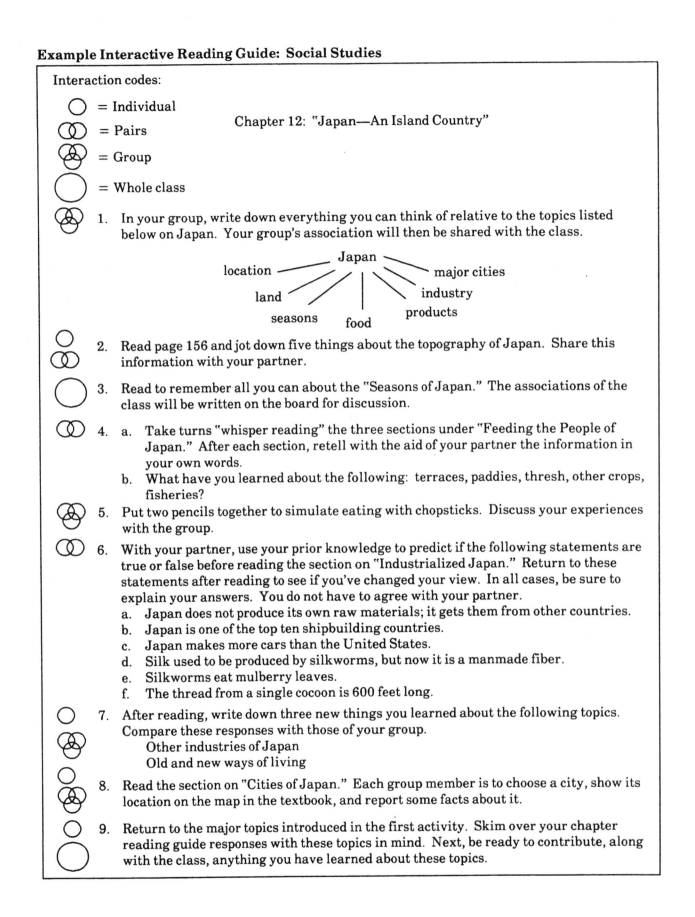

Interaction codes:

◯ = Individual

◑ = Pairs

◈ = Group

◯ = Whole class

Chapter 12: "Japan—An Island Country"

1. In your group, write down everything you can think of relative to the topics listed below on Japan. Your group's association will then be shared with the class.

location ——— Japan ——— major cities
land / | \ industry
seasons food products

2. Read page 156 and jot down five things about the topography of Japan. Share this information with your partner.

3. Read to remember all you can about the "Seasons of Japan." The associations of the class will be written on the board for discussion.

4. a. Take turns "whisper reading" the three sections under "Feeding the People of Japan." After each section, retell with the aid of your partner the information in your own words.
   b. What have you learned about the following: terraces, paddies, thresh, other crops, fisheries?

5. Put two pencils together to simulate eating with chopsticks. Discuss your experiences with the group.

6. With your partner, use your prior knowledge to predict if the following statements are true or false before reading the section on "Industrialized Japan." Return to these statements after reading to see if you've changed your view. In all cases, be sure to explain your answers. You do not have to agree with your partner.
   a. Japan does not produce its own raw materials; it gets them from other countries.
   b. Japan is one of the top ten shipbuilding countries.
   c. Japan makes more cars than the United States.
   d. Silk used to be produced by silkworms, but now it is a manmade fiber.
   e. Silkworms eat mulberry leaves.
   f. The thread from a single cocoon is 600 feet long.

7. After reading, write down three new things you learned about the following topics. Compare these responses with those of your group.
   Other industries of Japan
   Old and new ways of living

8. Read the section on "Cities of Japan." Each group member is to choose a city, show its location on the map in the textbook, and report some facts about it.

9. Return to the major topics introduced in the first activity. Skim over your chapter reading guide responses with these topics in mind. Next, be ready to contribute, along with the class, anything you have learned about these topics.

Re Quest

Description

Re Quest is a strategy that fosters active, rather than passive, reading of a text. The strategy provides a structure for students to ask questions about the reading. Both teachers and students take turns asking each other about common portions of an assigned reading. The teacher models good questioning behavior so that the students are able to create their own questions. Re Quest has several benefits.

- It encourages students to ask their own questions about assigned content material.
- It helps students establish a purpose for their reading.
- It fosters an active search for meaning.
- It develops independent comprehension abilities.
- It encourages students to hypothesize.

Procedure

Step 1: Both students and teacher silently read a segment of the text selection. (The segment length may range from one sentence to several paragraphs.)

Step 2: The teacher closes the book, and students ask questions about the passage.

Step 3: The teacher questions the students about the material, modeling good questioning behavior.

Step 4: Read the next segment of text, and repeat Steps 2 and 3.

Step 5: The exchange of questions stops when students have processed enough information to make predictions about the remainder of the assignment.

Step 6: Read the rest of the text silently to verify predictions.

Step 7: The teacher facilitates follow-up discussion of the material by having students compare their predictions with the text outcome.

Reference

Manzo, Tony V. "The Re Quest Procedure." *Journal of Reading* (November 1969), pp. 123-126.

Reciprocal Teaching

Description

Reciprocal Teaching is an instructional activity in the form of an interactive dialogue between the teacher and students regarding segments of text. The dialogue involves four strategies: summarizing, question generating, clarifying, and predicting. After the teacher models reading a passage and demonstrates each of the strategies, students take turns assuming the role of the discussion leader. The teacher then guides the process by providing appropriate feedback and support until the students have learned the process.

The discussion leader uses the four strategies to focus the discussion. Each strategy requires a different type of understanding. Summarizing requires students to restate what they've read in their own words. Question generating involves students in asking questions about the passage. Clarifying helps students focus on what makes a passage difficult to understand. Predicting encourages students to speculate about what will be discussed next in the text.

For reciprocal teaching to be effectively used in a classroom, several considerations need to be addressed.

- To prepare students for the activity, discuss the difficulties of the text and the reasons for adopting a strategic approach to reading textbook material.
- Give students an overview of the procedure, possibly by taking the role of discussion leader and guiding the class through the process.
- Allow time for students to practice each of the strategies so that they learn them or refresh their memories.
- Once students become familiar with the strategies, demonstrate the whole procedure again. In the initial uses of reciprocal teaching, the teacher plays a very prominent role. As the students become more familiar with the procedure, the teacher's role diminishes.

Procedure

Step 1: Students and the teacher read the selection individually.

Step 2: Rather than becoming involved in a teacher-led discussion, the students and the teacher take turns leading the discussion of the selection.

Step 3: Each discussion leader prepares to lead the discussion on a particular segment of text by creating a summary, generating a question to ask, locating potentially troublesome vocabulary or concepts, and deciding on a prediction to make.

Step 4: Other class members may add to the discussion by commenting on the summary, answering the question, clarifying vocabulary or asking to have vocabulary clarified, and making predictions. The teacher makes similar comments.

Summarizing

Students restate what they've read in their own words. Through summarizing, students work to find the most important information in the text. Initially, their summaries may be of sentences or paragraphs. Gradually, the summaries should focus on larger units of text.

Question Generating

Students ask questions about the passage. In order to do so, they must identify significant information, pose questions related to this information, and check to make sure they can answer their own questions. These questions help the student asking the question and the others to understand the passage.

Clarifying

Clarifying helps students focus on what makes a passage difficult to understand. For example, passages pose difficulty because of new vocabulary, unclear referents, or new concepts. Students may choose to either clarify a word or concept or identify a word or concept that needs to be clarified.

Predicting

With predicting, students speculate what will be discussed next in the text. To be successful, students must recall relevant background knowledge. Prediction helps set purposes for reading and affords an opportunity for students to connect what they are reading with what they know.

Example: Science

The following example of reciprocal teaching is set in a fourth-grade science classroom. The students have just read a passage called, "A Board and Block Lift Things," on the topic of levers.

Student Leader: The reading is about a kind of machine called a lever. (This is the student's summary.)
Student A: The lever helps you lift things.
Student Leader: My question is whether I could lift the teacher using a lever. (This student's question relates to interest; other questions could focus more on concepts.)
Student B: I have a question, too. How does a lever work? Is there a trick?
Student Leader: I'm not sure. I think a long board helps it work. The hardest word for me is fulcrum. I think it means the piece of wood the lever sits upon. (The student is both trying to clarify a word and possibly asking for further clarification.)
Student A: I think a fulcrum makes it like a teeter-totter. It's the middle part. But I don't know how it works.
Student B: If you move the block of wood in the middle, you can't pick up anything heavy. If you move it to the end you can.
Student Leader: I think we could lift the teacher if we used a lever. (This is the student's prediction.)
Student C: I don't think we can. She's too heavy for me to lift.
Student B: We could if we had a long board.
Teacher: Perhaps it makes a difference where we put the fulcrum.
Student A: We want the fulcrum real close to the teacher so we can lift him/her.

The reciprocal teaching would continue, with other students taking over the role of leader. The teacher would participate to help the discussion develop. While the teacher may feel a need to focus the discussion or to correct misunderstandings, the teacher should encourage the student leaders to do the focusing when possible.

References

Palincsar, A. S. "Reciprocal Teaching." In *Strategies for Teaching Reading as Thinking, A Tele-conference Resource Guide*. Elmhurst, IL: North Central Regional Education Laboratory, Feb. 11, 1988.

Reading from Different Perspectives

Description

A reader's perspective and background knowledge on a topic significantly influence how a specific text is understood and interpreted. Reading from Different Perspectives, a strategy that guides students through repeated readings of a selection, helps them discover alternative ways to interpret a particular reading.

For example, students initially may read a social studies textbook passage on the Reconstruction to find out what happened during this period in American history. Students could broaden their understanding of the era if they read the passage a second time from the perspective of a recently freed slave. By directing students to look at the text in a different way, teachers help students gain new insights into the concepts being taught. Reading from Different Perspectives helps students develop critical reading skills as they become aware of multiple interpretations of a reading. This strategy expands student comprehension from what were narrow interpretations. Reading from Different Perspectives, therefore, provides students with meaningful reasons to reread a selection.

Procedure

Step 1: Select one story, article, or book. Have the students first read it to get the gist of the material.

Step 2: Identify a number of perspectives related to important concepts and ideas in the reading. List them on the chalkboard or an overhead transparency. For instance, after reading an article on acid rain, students could reread the selection from one of the following perspectives: a fish, a fisherman, the lake, a resort owner, or the president of an electric utility. Various selections can be reread from the perspectives of different social or economic roles—father, mother, sister, doctor, labor union member, or governor. Some materials may lend themselves to perspectives from different theoretical or political positions—Marxist, Freudian, environmentalist, Republican, Libertarian.

Step 3: Model how a person from one of these perspectives would react to the materials the students have just read. You also may wish to demonstrate how a person with a given perspective would respond to a variety of situations.

Step 4: Divide the class into small groups and assign each group a perspective that they will assume as they reread the selection.

Step 5: Guide each group as they define the concerns and needs that someone of their assigned perspective would have on the topic. Assist students as they complete their perspective guide by listing the most important concerns and needs for their assigned perspective.

Step 6: As students reread the passage, have them identify text statements that are most important to their assigned perspective. Guide students in listing these statements and their reactions based on their perspectives.

Step 7: Guide students as they determine whether there is any information missing from the selection that would be important to them.

Step 8: Discuss with the entire class the insights that students gained through their rereading based on different perspectives. Students then may be instructed to write a summary position statement on both the text information and the different perspectives.

Sample Reading from Different Perspectives Guide

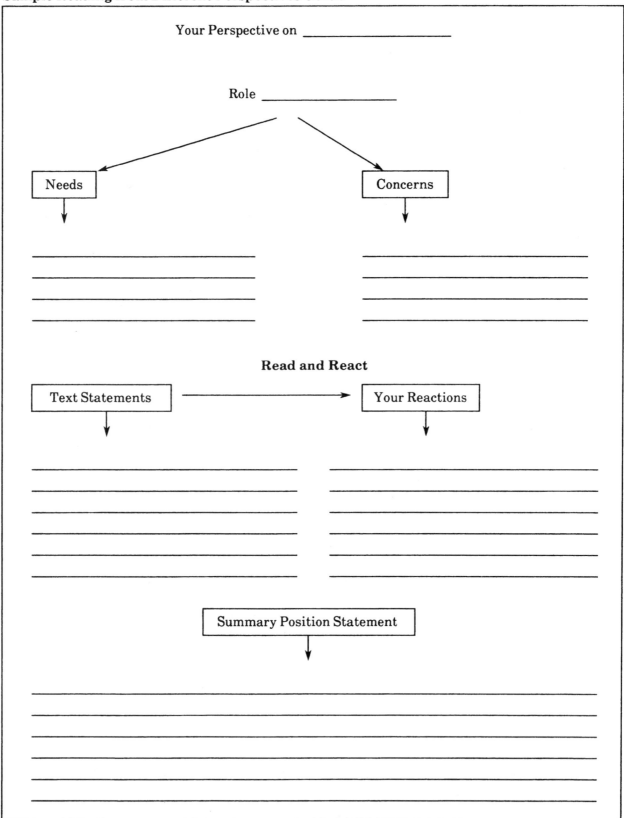

Example: Reading from Different Perspectives Guide for Social Studies

Your Perspective on <u>Declaration of Independence</u>

(Possible Roles: Share owner, English Governor of Massachusetts, 34-year-old
indentured servant, colonial patriot, colonial wife)

Role <u>King George</u>

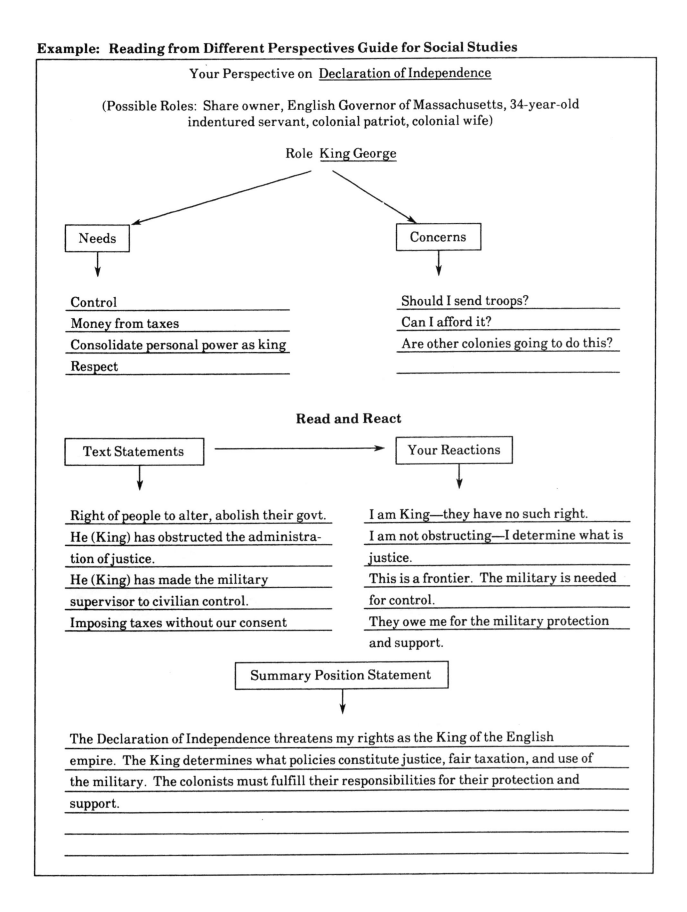

Needs	Concerns

Control

Money from taxes

Consolidate personal power as king

Respect

Should I send troops?

Can I afford it?

Are other colonies going to do this?

Read and React

Text Statements	→	Your Reactions

Right of people to alter, abolish their govt.

He (King) has obstructed the administration of justice.

He (King) has made the military supervisor to civilian control.

Imposing taxes without our consent

I am King—they have no such right.

I am not obstructing—I determine what is justice.

This is a frontier. The military is needed for control.

They owe me for the military protection and support.

Summary Position Statement

The Declaration of Independence threatens my rights as the King of the English
empire. The King determines what policies constitute justice, fair taxation, and use of
the military. The colonists must fulfill their responsibilities for their protection and
support.

Reference

McNeil, John D., *Reading Comprehension: New Directions for Classroom Practice*. Glenview, IL: Scott, Foresman, 1984.

RAFT

Description

The RAFT technique provides an easy, meaningful way to incorporate writing into content-area instruction. It includes the following four components:

R: Role of Writer—Who are you? A principal, Beethoven, a human heart?
A: Audience—To whom is this written? A corporation, a scientist, a lawyer?
F: Format—What form will it take? A letter, a poem, a journal?
T: Topic + Strong Verb—What important topic have I chosen? Choose a strong verb to describe your intent: persuade a corporation to accept your invention; demand payment for an injury; plead for leniency.

RAFT is especially effective because students write to an audience different from the teacher, and they write for a specific purpose. Because the writing is specific and well-focused, students understand the need to explain the topic clearly and completely.

The technique offers boundless opportunities for students to apply knowledge learned in content-area classrooms as they lead discussions, convince the class, or clarify a viewpoint. Teachers who have used RAFT report that the technique actually helps students learn more content. RAFT writing assignments also can be used at the beginning of a lesson to determine the students' background knowledge.

Procedure

Step 1: Explain that all writers need to consider four components of every composition: role of writer, audience, format, and topic.
Step 2: Brainstorm ideas about a topic. Select several topics from those mentioned.
Step 3: Write RAFT on the board, and list possible roles, audiences, formats, and strong verbs that are appropriate for each topic.
Step 4: Have students choose one of the examples to write about; or after discussing a topic, have students create their own RAFT writing assignment.

Example 1: Mathematics RAFT Paper

R: point
A: teacher
F: letter
T: convince the teacher that you have an important function

Dear Mrs. Havens,

I am Pete, the point. I am one point of an endless number of points in space. I want to ask you if you will teach your students about us points and explain how every single geometric figure is made up of us. It is very important to me because it seems that many people think of the point as a small part of geometry since we are so little. Though we are little, we are one of the most important factors of our world of geometry. Without me and all other points, there would be no geometric figures. We are their building blocks. Though all lines are drawn with one solid mark, in reality, a line is an endless set of points going in opposite directions. A sphere is a figure with all points at an equal distance from a center point like me.

So please, tell your students all about us points. It troubles me when many think of us as unimportant specks in space. Please, spread the reality of our importance to the students you teach. My partners and I would appreciate it greatly. Thank you.

A point,

Pete

Source: Janice Strop, Wisconsin CRISS workshops.

Example 2: Possible RAFT Writing Activities

Role	Audience	Format	Topic
citizen	Dem., Rep. or legislator	letter	Vote for recycling.
student	Japanese prime minister	letter	Persuade Japanese to stop killing whales for research purposes.
columnist Mike Royko	public	news column	Demand more gun control.
constituent	U.S. senator	letter	Plead to abolish capital punishment.
chemist	chemical company	instructions	Warn about combinations to avoid.
cracker	other crackers	travel guide	Journey through digestive system.
plant	sun	thank you note	Explain sun's role in plant's growth.
newswriter	public	news release	Explain how ozone layer was formed.
scientist	Charles Darwin	letter	Refute a point in evolution theory.
square root	whole number	love letter	Explain a relationship.
trout	self	diary	Desrcibe effects of acid rain on lake
criminal	judge	plea	Explain why he shouldn't be punished
acute triangle	obtuse triangle	article/letter	Convince obtuse triangle to shape up and lose weight. Explain differences.
leader of country	government of country	resume	Explain why she/he is a strong leader
animal	zookeeper	letter	Explain what I'll need when brought to zoo
Bolsheviks	peasants	advertisement	Convince peasants of better situations.
store owner	new employees	memo	Let employees know what kinds of math they will use in the store.
mineral	8th-grade science student	request, plea	Tell why every 8th-grade student should know me.
lungs	smoker	radio commercial	Convince person to stop smoking.
red blood cell traveling through circulatory system	new cells traveling through the system	dialogue	Warn of hazards on journey, including peer pressure of white blood cells.

Source: Janice Strop, Wisconsin CRISS workshops.

Reference

Santa, C. M. *Content Reading Including Secondary Systems*. Dubuque, IA: Kendall Hunt, 1988.

Framed Paragraphs

Description

Framed paragraphs are an excellent way to teach students about organizational patterns. By providing students with significant textual organizational cues, students are guided in their writing to recognize and use the frames that are appropriate to the material being studied. The following example shows how framed paragraphs guide students to write a well-formed paragraph using a problem/solution frame.

"A knowledge of the genetics of populations helps to solve many kinds of problems. This knowledge is important because _____

_____. *It also* _____

_____. *In addition,* _____

_____. *This knowledge has*

practical applications in medicine, education and government."

Framed paragraphs can be used in many content areas in a variety of ways. In addition to teaching text structure and paragraph writing skills, framed paragraphs can be adapted to

- review a previous lecture or discussion,
- provide class summaries for absent students,
- guide notetaking on lectures or films,
- develop skill in answering essay questions,
- encourage higher-level thinking skills.

Framed paragraphs help students write well-formed paragraphs. Gradually, as students gain confidence in writing, frames are no longer necessary.

Procedure

Step 1. Identify the text frame (problem/solution, compare/contrast, cause/effect, sequential, proposition/support) that represents the organization of the material.

Step 2. Provide part or all of a topic sentence. This can be located any place in the paragraph and should indicate the frame to be constructed.

Step 3. Indicate the beginnings of three to five sentences that will develop the topic sentence.

Step 4. Provide appropriate transitions when needed. The following is a partial list of useful transitions for framed paragraphs.

- main idea/detail: *moreover, furthermore, besides, then, first, second, finally, last*
- comparison: *similarly, likewise, in like manner*
- contrast: *but, yet, however, on the other hand, on the contrary, notwithstanding*

- conclusion: *therefore, accordingly, thus*
- time: *immediately, soon, after a few days, afterward*

Step 5. Provide all or part of a concluding sentence or summary.
Step 6. Encourage a variety of sentence lengths and formats.

References

Nichols, James. "Using Paragraph Frames to Help Remedial High School Students with Written Assignments." *Journal of Reading* (December 1980), pp. 228-231.

Santa, C.M. "Framed Paragraphs," In *Content Reading Including Secondary Systems*. Dubuque, IA: Kendall Hunt, 1988, pp. 13-15.

Framed Paragraph Examples

Example 1: Character Analysis

_____ is an important character in our story. _____ is important

because _____

_____ . Once, he/she _____

_____ . Another time,_____

_____ . I think that _____

                                                                                (character's name)

is _____

                            (character trait)

because _____

Example 2: Lab Report

1. Lab activity title:

2. Date:

3. The purpose of the lab is to . . . .

4. My hypothesis of what the results will be is . . . .

5. Data . . .

6. The data show . . .

7. After class discussion, I found my data was right/wrong. If wrong, what might have caused the error?

8. My final conclusion is . . . (If different from #6)

9. Answers to teacher or book provided questions:

Example 3: Essay Writing

Introductory Paragraph

Sentence 1 summarizes what your essay will be about. An example that you can use follows.

"The First Amendment to the U.S. Constitution guarantees Americans many important freedoms."

Sentence 2 tells what part you have chosen.

"I believe that freedom _____ is
the most valuable part of the First Amendment."

Sentence 3 or more tells briefly why you think it is the most important.

"It is important because _____

_____
                                                              "

_____

Body Paragraphs

This paragraph explains your reasons more completely.

"The first reason I think the freedom _____ is
                                                                                    "
important is because _____

"Secondly, it is important because _____
                                                                                        "

_____

"Here is an example _____
                                                                                        "

_____

"Thirdly, because _____
                                                                                      "

_____

"The following shows how _____
                                                                                        "

_____

"Lastly, _____
                                                                                    "

_____

"This is an example of how this works. _____
                                                                                        "

_____

Concluding Paragraph

"Freedom _____, from the First
Amendment to the U.S. Constitution, has given Americans the right to _____
_____ and that is very important to me and our country.

Source: Nancy Roth, East High School, Madison (Wisconsin) Metropolitan School District, 1988.

The Four-Step Summary

Description

The Four-Step Summary writing procedure is a strategy that can be used to reinforce or apply what students have learned. Students get practice in distilling text into the most important information. The strategy involves creating a summary of four sentences, one for each step in the formula. The procedure also may be used to create a one-sentence summary.

Teachers can use summaries in many ways. They can be a variation on study guides, a comprehension check on homework, a statement of progress on a class project, a report on a class lecture, or a substitute for a quiz. The key to this cognitive-organizing process is the four-step formula. Students look at what they have to learn in terms of these four points of focus.

The Four-Step Formula

1. Identify the topic being summarized.
2. Tell what the passage begins with.
3. Tell what is covered in the middle (or what the passage is mostly about). Words and phrases such as "covers," "discusses," "presents," and "develops the idea that " are useful here.
4. Tell what the passage ends with.

Procedure

Step 1: Give students a copy of the "Steps in Writing a Summary" formula included in this section.

Step 2: Use familiar material, such as material students have already read and studied. On the chalkboard or overhead projector, write the information in the four columns, following the formula steps.

Step 3: Model how to put the information into sentences. Pay special attention to possible verbs that will connect the information. The sentences will almost write themselves.

Step 4: Guide students as they individually, in pairs, or in small groups complete their summaries of the new material.

Step 5: Model well-written summaries by writing student examples on the board. Discuss the construction of a well-written summary according to the guidelines on the handout.

Step 6: Challenge the most skilled students to write a one-sentence summary. Instruct them to add only one "and" as a conjunction, and advise them to use "ends with" for Step 4 in the fomula.

Steps in Writing a Summary

First, begin by making four columns on a sheet of paper.

What are you summarizing?	What does it begin with?	What is in the middle?	How does it end?

Second, fill in these columns with information from your reading. As you fill in the columns, remember to

1. delete trivial material,

2. delete repetitive material, and

3. provide a term that labels or categorizes a list of items or actions.

Third, when you have filled in your columns, write a summary sentence using this information for each column. Or, instead of four sentences, put all the information into one sentence.

Fourth, ask yourself the following questions after you have written your summary:

1. Is anything important left out?

2. Is the information in the right order?

3. Have I selected to write the things that the author or teacher think are most important?

Finally, ask yourself about the style of writing.

1. Read each sentence aloud to be sure it reads smoothly.

2. How easy is it to read aloud?

3. Can I change words to smooth it out?

4. Have I used any unnecessary words?

If you have accomplished all these steps, you probably have written a pretty good Four-Step Summary.

Examples of One-Sentence Summaries

Example 1: Science

The section on "Ocean Life Zones" begins with listing the factors that affect ocean life, then classifies ocean life into three groups by their habits and depth of ocean water in which they live, and ends with a description of three kinds of ocean life: plankton, necton, and benthos.

Example 2: Literature

Shakespeare's play *Macbeth* begins with three witches setting the ominous tone of the play, delineates the changes in Macbeth's character resulting from overweening ambition, and ends when retribution against Macbeth brings the rightful king to the throne.

Reference

Stanfill, Silver. "The Great American One-Sentence Summary." In *Classroom Practices in Teaching Classroom English*. Urbana, IL: National Council of Teachers of English, 1978, pp. 47-49.

Appendixes 10

Metacognitive instruction differs from study skills instruction in that it teaches students to monitor their own comprehension, to understand the underlying purposes of various study methods and to select an appropriate method independently.
—Michigan

Annotated Bibliography

Dimensions of Thinking: A Framework for Curriculum and Instruction, ed. by R. Marzano, et al. Alexandria, VA: Association for Supervision and Curriculum Development, 1988.

The authors of this book describe what it means to "teach thinking" and how schools can prepare for it. They have developed a powerful, yet flexible framework focusing on five dimensions of thinking: metacognition, critical and creative thinking, thinking processes, core thinking, and the relationship of content-area knowledge to thinking. The framework serves as a basis for both curriculum and staff development programs. The authors have organized and clarified research and theory from several sources so that it is useful to practitioners who want to integrate the teaching of thinking with regular academic instruction. This book moves our understanding of thinking beyond just detailed lists of thinking skills and challenges traditional notions about purposes and methods of instruction. In so doing, it considers the implications of teaching thinking on such problems as student failure and unmet potential. The book has implications for preservice and inservice teachers and for refocusing the efforts of supervisors, principals, and boards of education.

Prereading Activities for Content Area Reading and Learning, 2nd ed., by D.W. Moore, J.E. Readance, and R.J. Rickelman. Newark, DE: International Reading Association, 1989.

The premise of this book is that what students know before they read will strongly influence what they learn by reading. The authors have drawn from many sources to assemble a collection of instructional options for preparing students to read their texts in different content areas. The options are practical in content-area classes and productive because they enhance students' learning. The text describes specific prereading activities and presents considerations for selecting or designing prereading techniques.

Reading Activities in Content Areas, 3rd ed., by R. Pavlik and D. Piercey. Newton, MA: Allyn and Bacon, in press.

The third edition contains hundreds of content area reading activities, based on the reader-text-content model of comprehension. The activities are organized and cross-referenced according to the interactions of strategic readers, a variety of reading texts, and more than 30 subjects.

The Reading Report Card: Progress Toward Excellence in Our Schools, compiled by National Assessment of Educational Progress. Princeton, NJ: Educational Testing Service, 1985.

This report focuses on trends in reading achievement for U.S. school children from 1970 to 1984. It describes how well nine-, thirteen-, and in-school seventeen-year-olds can read and considers the relationships between reading achievement, television viewing, and amount of homework.

Reading, Thinking, and Concept Development: Strategies for the Classroom, ed. by T.L. Harris and E.J. Cooper. New York: College Board, 1985.

This is a collection of 15 original articles, written by some of the nation's leading educators, that speak to the teaching of reading as thinking. The articles stress instruction in comprehension and thinking at the elementary and secondary levels and across subject areas. The authors explain not only how to foster comprehension processes but also why the procedures work. Strategies presented are prescriptive, outlining specific ways of processing text to achieve certain comprehension and cognitive goals. The book stresses the relationship of process to content, focusing on the dynamics of the teaching-learning situation. Topics in the book include explicit, interactive, integrative comprehension strategies and the future use of textbooks.

Research Within Reach: Secondary School Reading, ed. by D.E. Alvermann, D.W. Moore, and M.W. Conley. Newark, DE: International Reading Association, 1987.
This volume synthesizes and translates research on secondary reading so that the best information at that level is available to classroom teachers. The book contains five chapters: knowing why, knowing what, knowing how, knowing when, and knowing who. Each chapter asks questions about secondary school reading, provides research-based answers, and concludes with a summary and references. The book is designed to heighten teacher awareness of the need for change and to provide some answers to questions that secondary school teachers often ask about learning.

Strategic Teaching and Learning: Cognitive Instruction in the Content Areas, ed. by B.F. Jones, A.S. Palincsar, D.S. Ogle, and E.G. Carr. Alexandria, VA: Association for Supervision and Curriculum Development, 1987.
This book emphasizes the teacher's role in planning and mediating learning. In this role, the teacher teaches the content as well as the strategies required by the content to make learning meaningful, integrated, and transferable. Strategic teaching is a demanding concept. Teachers must know the content thoroughly; assess their student's prior knowledge and learning needs; analyze textbooks and other instructional materials; understand students' thinking; and match students, texts, and strategies. The book specifically presents applications of strategic thinking in each of the major content areas.

Teaching Thinking Skills: English/Language Arts, ed. by B.F. Jones, M.B. Tinzmann, L.B. Friedman, and B.B. Walker. Washington, DC: National Education Association, 1987.
This book responds to the growing interest among content teachers in teaching language arts skills (especially comprehension and writing) across the curriculum. The book provides a framework for teaching language arts across the curriculum. It integrates research on learning and instruction in each of the language arts as well as research on the organizational patterns found in literature and content texts. The authors emphasize three major themes: (1) the learner works actively to construct meaning, (2) the goals of instruction involve both understanding the content and becoming an independent learner, and (3) the learner must link new information to prior knowledge.

Who Reads Best? Factors Related to Reading Achievement in Grades 3, 7, and 11, ed. by A.N. Applebee, J.A. Langer, and I.V.S. Mullis. Princeton, NJ: Educational Testing Service, 1988.
This report, based on NAEP's 1985 national assessment of reading achievement (see *The Reading Report Card* above), describes the characteristics and attitudes of na-

tionally representative samples of students in relation to how well they can read. It details the specific features of reading instruction, how students approach their reading tasks, student reading experiences, and home and school supports for academic achievement. Major findings document changes in reading instruction, showing a movement away from an overwhelming emphasis on basals and workbooks and toward a greater emphasis on comprehension strategies, a wider range of reading materials, more independent reading, and more integration of reading and writing.

Bibliography

Adams, M., and B. Bruce. "Background Knowledge and Reading Comprehension." In *Reader Meets Author/Bridging the Gap: A Psycholinguistic and Sociolinguistic Perspective*, edited by J. Langer and M.T. Smith-Burke. Newark, DE: International Reading Association, 1982.

Alvermann, D.E. "Strategic Teaching in Social Studies." In *Strategic Teaching and Learning*, edited by B.F. Jones, A.S. Palincsar, D.S. Ogle, and E.G. Carr. Alexandria, VA: Association for Supervision and Curriculum Development, 1987.

Alvermann, D.E., D.W. Moore, and M.W. Conley, eds. *Research Within Reach: Secondary School Reading*. Newark, DE: International Reading Association, 1987.

Anderson, C.W. "Strategic Teaching in Science." In *Strategic Teaching and Learning*, edited by B.F. Jones, A.S. Palincsar, D.S. Ogle, and E.G. Carr. Alexandria, VA: Association for Supervision and Curriculum Development, 1987.

Anderson, C.W., and E.L. Smith. "Children's Preconceptions and Content-Area Textbooks." In *Comprehension Instruction: Perspectives and Suggestions*, edited by G. Duffy, L. Roehler, and J. Mason. New York: Longman, 1984.

Anderson, R.C. "The Notion of Schemata and the Educational Enterprise." In *Schooling and the Acquisition of Knowledge*, edited by J. Spiro and W.E. Montague. Hillsdale, NJ: Erlbaum, 1977.

Anderson, R.C., and W. Biddle. "On Asking People Questions About What They Are Reading." In *The Psychology of Learning and Motivation*, edited by G. Bower. New York: Academic Press, 1975.

Anderson, R.C., E.H. Hiebert, J.A. Scott, and I. Wilkinson. *Becoming a Nation of Readers*. Champaign: University of Illinois, Center for the Study of Reading, 1985.

Anderson, R.C., and J.W. Pichert. "Recall of Previously Unrecallable Information Following a Shift in Perspective." *Journal of Verbal Learning and Verbal Behavior* 17 (1978).

Anderson, R.C., R.E. Reynolds, D.C. Schallert, and E.T. Goetz. "Frameworks for Comprehending Discourse." *American Education Research Journal* 14 (1977).

Anderson, T.H., B.B. Armbruster, and R.N. Kantor. *How Clearly Written Are Children's Textbooks? Or, of Bladderworts and Alfa.* (Reading Education Report No. 16). Champaign: University of Illinois, Center for the Study of Reading, 1980.

Andre, M.D.A., and T.H. Anderson. "The Development and Evaluation of a Self-Questioning Study Technique." *Reading Research Quarterly* 14 (1979).

Armbruster, B.B., and T.H. Anderson. *Producing "Considerate" Expository Text. Or, Easy Reading Is Damned Hard Writing.* (Reading Education Report No. 46). Champaign: University of Illinois, Center for the Study of Reading, 1984.

Baker, Linda, and Ann Brown. "Metacognitive Skills and Reading." In *Handbook of Reading Research*, edited by P.D. Pearson. New York: Longman, 1984.

Bartlett, B.J. "Top-Level Structure as an Organizational Strategy for Recall of Classroom Text." Ph.D. dissertation, Arizona State University, 1978.

Baumann, J.F. "Direct Instruction Reconsidered." *Journal of Reading* 31 (1988).

Beach, R. "Strategic Teaching in Literature." In *Strategic Teaching and Learning*, edited by B.F. Jones, A.S. Palincsar, D.S. Ogle, and E.G. Carr. Alexandria, VA: Association for Supervision and Curriculum Development, 1987.

Beck, I.L., C.A. Perfetti, and M.G. McKeown. "Effects of Long-Term Vocabulary Instruction on Lexical Access and Reading Comprehension." *Journal of Educational Psychology* 74 (1982).

Bereiter, C., and M. Scardamalia. "Reconstruction of Cognitive Skills." Paper read at the annual meeting of the American Educational Research Association, New Orleans, 1984.

Berger, A., and H.A. Robinson. *Secondary School Reading: What Research Reveals for Classroom Practice.* Urbana, IL: North Central Regional Educational Laboratory, 1982.

Blanton, W.E., and G.B. Moorman. "The Information Text Reading Activity (ITRA): Engaging Students in Meaningful Learning from Text." Paper read at the International Reading Association Convention, Anaheim, CA, 1987.

_____. "Research Relevant to Learning from Information Text." Paper read at the International Reading Association Convention , Anaheim, CA, 1987.

Bower, G. H. "Organizational Factors in Meaning." *Cognitive Psychology* 1 (1970).

Bragaw, D., and H.M. Hartoonian. "Social Studies: The Study of People in Society." In *1988 Association for Supervision and Curriculum Development Yearbook*, edited by Ronald S. Brandt. Alexandria, VA: Association for Supervision and Curriculum Development, 1988.

Bragstad, B., and S. Stumpf. *A Guidebook for Teaching Study Skills and Motivation.* 2nd ed. Newton, MA: Allyn and Bacon, 1987.

Bransford, J.D., B.S. Stein, T.S. Shelton, and R.A. Owings. "Cognitions and Adaptation: The Importance of Learning to Learn." In *Cognition, Social Behavior and the Environment*, edited by J. Harvey. Hillsdale, NJ: Erlbaum, 1980.

Brown, A.L., J.C. Campione , and J. Day. "Learning to Learn: On Training Students to Learn from Texts." *Educational Researcher* 10 (1981).

Brown, A.L., and A.S. Palincsar. "Inducing Strategic Learning from Texts by Means of Informed, Self-Control Training." *Topics in Learning and Learning Disabilities* 2 (1982).

Brown, Ann. "Metacognitive Development and Reading." In *Theoretical Issues in Reading Comprehension*, edited by R.J. Spiro, B.C. Bruce, and W.F. Brewer. Hillsdale, NJ: Erlbaum, 1980.

Buehl, D., G. Cook, K. Ehlert, and D. Vance. "New Perspectives in Effecting Change: Using Newsletters to Inservice Content Teachers." *WSRA Journal* 30 (1986).

Capper, Joanne. "Research in Science Education: A Cognitive Science Perspective." In *The Research Digest*. Washington, DC: Center for Research into Practice, 1984.

Carpenter, T.P. "Learning to Add and Subtract: An Exercise in Problem Solving." In *Teaching and Learning Mathematical Problem Solving*, edited by E.A. Silver. Hillsdale, NJ: Erlbaum, 1985.

Cohen, P.A., J.A. Kulik, and C.C. Kulik. "Educational Outcomes of Tutoring: A Meta-Analysis of Findings." *American Educational Research Journal* 19 (1982).

Cohen, R. "Self-Generated Questions as an Aid to Reading Comprehension." *The Reading Teacher* 36 (1983).

Cole, W. "Delivery Systems in Staff Development: When, Who, and Where." In *Adapting Educational Research: Staff Development Approaches*, edited by L. Morris. Norman: University of Oklahoma, Teacher Corps Research Adaptation Cluster, 1979.

Craik, F.I.M., and R.S. Lockhart. "Levels of Processing: A Framework for Memory Research." *Journal of Verbal Learning and Verbal Behavior* 11 (1972).

Dansereau, D.F. "Transfer from Cooperative to Individual Studying." *Journal of Reading* 30 (1987).

Doctorow, M., M.C. Wittrock, and C. Marks. "Generative Processes in Reading Comprehension." *Journal of Educational Psychology* 70 (1978).

Duffy, G.G., and L.R. Roehler. *Improving Classroom Reading Instruction*. New York: Random House, 1986.

Dupuis, M., ed. *Reading in the Content Areas: Research for Teachers*. Newark, DE: International Reading Association, 1984.

Dupuis, M., and E.N. Askov. *Content Area Reading.* Englewood Cliffs, NJ: Prentice-Hall, 1982.

Durkin, D. "What Classroom Observations Reveal About Reading Comprehension Instruction." *Reading Research Quarterly* 14 (1978).

Edeburn, C.E., and R.G. Landry. "Teacher Self-Concept and Student Self-Concept in Grades Three, Four, and Five." *Journal of Educational Research* 69 (1976).

Fagan, E.R., D.M. Hassler, and M. Szabo. "Evaluation of Questioning Strategies in Language Arts Instruction." *Research in the Teaching of English* 15 (1981).

Fass, W., and G.M. Schumacker. "Schema Theory and Prose Retention: Boundary Conditions for Encoding and Retrieval Effects." *Discourse Processes* 4 (1981).

Flavell, J.H. "Metacognitive Development." In *Structural Process Theories of Complex Human Behavior,* edited by J. M. Scandura and C. J. Brainerd. Alphen a. d. Rijn, the Netherlands: Sijthoff and Noordhoff, 1978.

Flavell, J.H., and H.M. Wellman. "Metamemory." In *Perspective on the Development of Memory and Cognition,* edited by R.V. Kail Jr., and J.W. Hagen. Hillsdale, NJ: Erlbaum, 1977.

Frase, L.T., and B.J. Schwartz. "Effect of Question Production and Answering on Prose Recall." *Journal of Educational Psychology* 67 (1975).

Frederiksen, C.H. "Acquisition of Semantic Information from Discourse: Effects of Repeated Exposures." *Journal of Verbal Learning and Verbal Behavior* 14 (1975).

"Representing Logical and Semantic Structure of Knowledge Acquired from Discourse." *Cognitive Psychology* 7 (1975).

Gall, M.D., et al. *The Effects of Teacher Use of Questioning Techniques on Student Achievement and Attitude.* San Francisco: Far West Laboratory for Educational Research and Development, 1975.

Goetz, E.T., R.E. Reynolds, D.L. Shallert, and D.I. Radin. "Reading in Perspective: What Real Cops and Pretend Burglars Look for in a Story." *Journal of Educational Psychology* 75 (1983).

Goodlad, J. *A Place Called School.* New York: McGraw-Hill, 1983.

Goodman, Y., and C. Burke. *Reading Miscue Inventory Manual.* New York: MacMillan, 1970.

Hall, G.E., and S.M. Hord. *Change in Schools: Facilitating the Process.* Albany: State University of New York Press, 1988.

Harris, T.L., and E.J. Cooper, eds. *Reading, Thinking, and Concept Development: Strategies for the Classroom.* New York: College Board, 1985.

Hartoonian, H. M. "Content For Thinking: Academic Subject Areas and Principles of Reasoning." In *Teachers Tackle Thinking*, edited by D.R. Claseu and C. Bonk. Madison: University of Wisconsin Extension Press, 1988.

Heimlich, J.E., and S.D. Pittelman. *Semantic Mapping: Classroom Applications*. Newark, DE: International Reading Association, 1986.

Herber, H., and J. Nelson-Herber. "Developing Independent Learners." *Journal of Reading* 30 (1987).

_____. "Planning the Program." In *Becoming Readers in a Complex Society*, edited by O. Niles and A. Purves. Chicago: University of Chicago Press, 1984.

Herman, P., R.C. Anderson, P.D. Pearson, and W. Nagy. *Incidental Learning of Word Meanings from Expositions That Systematically Vary Text Features*. (Technical Report No. 364). Champaign: University of Illinois, Center for the Study of Reading, 1985.

Howie, Sherry H. *A Guidebook for Teaching Writing in Content Areas*. Newton, MA: Allyn and Bacon, 1984.

Irwin, J.W., and C. A. Davis. "Assessing Readability: The Checklist Approach." *Journal of Reading* 24 (1980).

Johnson, D.D., S. Toms-Bronowski, and S.D. Pittelman. *An Investigation of the Trends in Vocabulary Research and the Effects of Prior Knowledge on Instructional Strategies for Vocabulary Acquisition*. (Theoretical Paper No. 95). Madison: Wisconsin Center for Educational Research, 1981.

Johnson, D.W., and R.T. Johnson. *Learning Together and Alone*. Englewood Cliffs, NJ: Prentice-Hall, 1987.

Johnston, P., and P.D. Pearson. *Prior Knowledge, Connectivity and the Assessment of Reading Comprehension*. (Technical Report No. 245). Champaign: University of Illinois, Center for the Study of Reading, 1982.

Johnston, P., and P. Winograd. "Passive Failure in Reading." *Journal of Reading Behavior* 17 (1985).

Jones, B.F., A.S. Palincsar, D.S. Ogle, and E.G. Carr, eds. *Strategic Teaching and Learning: Cognitive Instruction in the Content Areas*. Alexandria, VA: Association for Supervision and Curriculum Development, 1987.

Jones, B.F., J. Pierce, and B. Hunter. "Teaching Students to Construct Graphic Representations." *Educational Leadership*, 46 (1988).

_____. "Using Graphic Representations as a Strategy for Analysis and Problem Solving." Paper submitted to the Association for Supervision and Curriculum Development, 1988.

Jones, B.F., M.B. Tinzmann, L.B. Friedman, and B.B. Walker, eds. *Teaching Thinking Skills: English/Language Arts*. Washington, DC: National Education Association, 1987.

Joyce, B., and B. Showers. "The Coaching of Teaching." *Educational Leadership* 40 (1982).

_____. "Improving Inservice Training: The Messages of Research." *Educational Leadership* 37 (1980).

Kintsch, W., and T.A. Van Dijk. "Toward a Model of Text Comprehension and Production." *Psychological Review* 85 (1978).

Langer, J. "Examining Background Knowledge and Text Comprehension." *Reading Research Quarterly* 19 (1984).

Linden, M., and M.C. Wittrock. "The Teaching of Reading Comprehension According to the Model of Generative Learning." *Reading Research Quarterly* 17 (1981).

Lindquist, M.M. "Strategic Teaching in Mathematics." In *Strategic Teaching and Learning*, edited by B.F. Jones, A.S. Palincsar, D.S. Ogle, and E.G. Carr. Alexandria, VA: Association for Supervision and Curriculum Development, 1987.

Loftus, E. *Memory*. Reading, MA: Addison, Wesley, 1980.

Marshall, N., and M.D. Glock. "Comprehension of Connected Discourse: A Study into the Relationship Between the Structure of Text and Information Recalled." *Reading Research Quarterly* 14 (1979).

Marzano, R., et al., eds. *Dimensions of Thinking: A Framework for Curriculum and Instruction*. Alexandria, VA: Association for Supervision and Curriculum Development, 1988.

McClain-Ruelle, L.J. "Finessing Reading Strategies into the Secondary Content Classroom—An Inservice Delivery Model." *Reading Improvement* 25 (1988).

McNeil, John D. *Reading Comprehension: New Directions for Classroom Practice*. Glenview, IL: Scott Foresman, 1984.

Meyer, B.J.F. "Organizational Patterns in Prose and Their Use in Reading." In *Reading Research: Studies and Applications*, edited by M.L. Kamil and A.J. Moe. Clemson, SC: National Reading Conference, 1979.

_____. "The Structure of Text." In *Handbook of Reading Research*, edited by P.D. Pearson. New York: Longman, 1985.

Meyer, B.J.F., D.M. Brandt, and G.J. Bluth. "Use of Top-Level Structure in Text: Key for Reading Comprehension of Ninth-Grade Students." *Reading Research Quarterly* 15 (1980).

Moffett, J., and B.J. Wagner. *Student-Centered Language Arts and Reading, K-13: A Handbook for Teachers*. 3rd ed. Boston: Houghton Mifflin, 1983.

Mohlman, G., J. Kierstad, and M. Gunlach. "A Research-Based Inservice Model for Secondary Teachers." *Educational Leadership* 40 (1982).

Moore, D.W., J.E. Readence, and R.J. Rickelman. *Prereading Activities for Content Area Reading and Learning*. 2nd ed. Newark, DE: International Reading Association, 1989.

Myers, J. *Writing to Learn Across the Curriculum*. Bloomington, IN: Phi Delta Kappa, 1984.

Nagy, W. E., P.A. Herman, and R.C. Anderson. "The Inference of Word and Text Properties in Learning from Context." Paper read at the American Educational Research Association meeting, Chicago, 1985.

Nolan, J.F. "Reading in the Content Area of Mathematics." In *Reading in the Content Areas: Research for Teachers*, edited by M. Dupuis. Newark, DE: International Reading Association, 1984.

Palincsar, A.S., and A.L. Brown. "Reciprocal Teaching: Activities to Promote Reading With Your Mind." In *Reading, Thinking, and Concept Development: Strategies for the Classroom*, edited by T.L. Harris and E.J. Cogen. New York: College Board, 1985.

Paris, S.G., M.V. Lipson, and K. Wixson. "Becoming a Strategic Reader." *Contemporary Educational Psychology* 8 (1983).

Pauk, W. *How to Study in College*. 3rd ed. Boston: Houghton Mifflin, 1984.

Pavlik, R., and D. Piercey. *Reading Activities in the Content Areas*. Boston: Allyn and Bacon, 1989.

Pearson, P. D., "Twenty Years of Research in Comprehension." In *The Contexts of School-Based Literacy*, edited by T. Raphael. New York: Random House, 1987.

Pearson, P.D., and M.C. Gallagher. "The Instruction of Reading Comprehension." *Contemporary Educational Psychology* 8 (1983).

Quandt, I., and R. Selznick. *Self-Concept and Reading*. 2nd ed. Newark, DE: International Reading Association, 1984.

Raphael, T.E. *The Contexts of School-Based Literacy*. New York: Random House, 1987.

Readence, J.E., T. Bean, and R.S. Baldwin. *Content Area Reading: An Integrated Approach*. Dubuque, IA: Kendall Hunt, 1985.

Redfield, D.L., and E.W. Rousseau. "Meta-Analysis of Experimental Research on Teacher Questioning Behavior." *Review of Educational Research* 51 (1981).

Robinson, H.A. *Teaching Reading, Writing, and Study Strategies: The Content Areas.* 3rd ed. Boston: Allyn and Bacon, 1983.

Roth, K.J. "Conceptual Change Learning and Student Processing of Science Texts." Paper read at the American Educational Research Association meeting, Chicago, 1985.

Rowe, M.B. "Wait, Wait, Wait." *School Science and Mathematics* 78 (1978).

Rumelhart, D.E. "Schemata: The Building Blocks of Cognition." In *Theoretical Issues in Reading Comprehension*, edited by R.J. Spiro, B.C. Bruce, and W.F. Brewer. Hillsdale, NJ: Erlbaum, 1980.

Santa, C.M. *Content Reading Including Study Systems.* Dubuque, IA: Kendall Hunt, 1988.

Schacter, S.W. "An Investigation of the Effects of Vocabulary Instruction and Schemata Orientation on Reading Comprehension." Ph.D. dissertation, University of Minnesota, 1978.

Schoenfeld, A. H. *Mathematical Problem Solving.* New York: Academic Press, 1985.

Showers, B. *Transfer of Training: The Contribution of Coaching.* Eugene: University of Oregon, Center for Educational Policy and Management, 1984.

Slavin, R. "Cooperative Learning." *Review of Educational Research* 50 (1980).

_____. *Cooperative Learning: Student Teams.* Washington, DC: National Education Association, 1982.

Smith, C.F. "The Content Determines the Process: An Ignored Relationship in Content Area Reading." *WSRA Journal* 30 (1986).

Sparks, G. M. "The Effectiveness of Alternative Training Activities in Changing Teaching Practices." *American Educational Research Journal* 23 (1986).

Spiro, R.J. "Constructive Processes in Prose Comprehension and Recall." In *Theoretical Issues in Reading Comprehension*, edited by R.J. Spiro, B.C. Bruce, and W.F. Brewer. Hillsdale, NJ: Erlbaum, 1980.

Stevens, K. "Effects of Background Knowledge on the Reading Comprehension of Ninth Graders." *Journal of Reading Behavior* 12 (1980).

Tierney, Robert J., and James W. Cunningham. "Research on Teaching Reading Comprehension." In *Handbook of Reading Research*, edited by P.D. Pearson. New York: Longman, 1984.

Tierney, Robert J., and P.D. Pearson. "Toward a Composing Model." *Language Arts* 60 (1983).

Tobin, K. "The Role of Wait Time in Higher Cognitive Level Learning." *Review of Educational Research* 57 (1987).

Vacca, J.L. "Working with Content Area Teachers." In *Content Area Reading*, edited by R.T. Vacca and J.L. Vacca. Boston: Little, Brown, 1986.

Vacca, R.T., and J.L. Vacca. *Content Area Reading*. 2nd ed. Boston: Little, Brown, 1986.

Vygotsky, L.S. *Mind in Society: The Development of Higher Psychological Processes*. Cambridge, MA: Harvard University Press, 1978.

Weinstein, C. E. "Fostering Learning Autonomy Through the Use of Learning Strategies." *Journal of Reading* 30 (1987).

Wittrock, M.C., ed. *Handbook of Research on Teaching*. 3rd ed. New York: MacMillan, 1986.

_____. "Writing and Teaching of Reading." *Language Arts* 60 (1983).

Wixson, K. "Questions About a Text: What You Ask About Is What Children Learn." *The Reading Teacher* 37 (1983).

Resources

Association for Supervision and Curriculum
    Development (ASCD)
125 North West Street
Alexandria, VA 22314-2798
Tel. (703) 549-9110

Center for the Study of Reading
University of Illinois-Champaign
51 Gerty Drive
Champaign, IL 61820
Tel. (217) 333-2552

Center on Effective Secondary Schools
University of Wisconsin-Madison
Educational Sciences Building
1025 West Johnson Street
Madison, WI 53706
Tel. (608) 263-7575

Educational Resource Information
    Center (ERIC)
U.S. Department of Education
Office of Educational Research
    and Improvement
555 New Jersey Avenue, N.W.
Washington, DC 20208
Tel. (202) 357-6289

ERIC Clearinghouse on Reading and
    Communication Skills
Indiana University
Smith Research Center, Suite 150
2805 East Tenth Street
Bloomington, IN 47408
Tel. (812) 855-5847

International Reading Association
800 Barksdale Road
Box 8139
Newark, DE 19714-8139
Tel. (302) 731-1600

Michigan Reading Association
Box 7509
Grand Rapids, MI 49510
Tel. (616) 731-5617

North Central Regional Educational
    Laboratory
295 Emory Avenue
Elmhurst, IL 50126
Tel. (312) 941-7677

Orange County Schools
Box 271
Orlando, FL 32802
Tel. (407) 422-3200

Wisconsin State Reading Association
4809 Sternberg Avenue
Schofield, WI 54476
Tel. (414) 476-7320